Omelettes & Soufflés

ANNE BYRD

ILLUSTRATED BY DANA BURNS

HARPER & ROW, PUBLISHERS, New York

Cambridge, Philadelphia, San Francisco, London

Mexico City, São Paulo, Sydney

IRENA CHALMERS COOKBOOKS, INC., New York

For Carolyn Hines, my friend, editor and research assistant, in appreciation of a lifetime of friendship and years of professional assistance

OMELETTES & SOUFFLÉS. Copyright © 1982 by Anne Byrd. All rights reserved. Printed in the United States of America. No part of this book may be used or reproduced in any manner whatsoever without written permission except in the case of brief quotations embodied in critical articles and reviews. For information address Harper & Row, Publishers, Inc., 10 East 53rd Street, New York, N.Y. 10022. Published simultaneously in Canada by Fitzhenry & Whiteside Limited, Toronto.

FIRST HARPER & ROW EDITION

Library of Congress Cataloging in Publication Data

Byrd, Anne.
  Omelettes & soufflés.

  (Great American cooking schools series)
  1. Omelets. 2. Soufflés. I. Title. II. Title:
Omelettes and soufflés. III. Series.
TX745.B95 1982   641.8   82-47860
ISBN 0-06-015065-3

82 83 84 85 86 10 9 8 7 6 5 4 3 2 1

Contents

In Appreciation

This book is actually a joint venture. Without the assistance and support of my staff—Carolyn Banks, LaVenta Davis, Audrey Graham and Carolyn Hines—it would never have been completed. I thank them for their enthusiasm. I also thank my husband, Peter Gilchrist, who ate many eggs during the research and preparation of this book. His friendship and advice have guided me through this project as well as through many other endeavors.

In addition to those who worked closely with me on the book, there are several food professionals whose inspiration and information have been invaluable throughout my career. I would like to thank and acknowledge each of them: Irena Chalmers, my former cooking teacher and the publisher of this book, for her culinary instruction and for her advice on *Omelettes and Soufflés;* Father Robert Farrar Capon, mentor of my soul and palate, for his influence on my life and my writing; Nathalie Dupree, friend and colleague, for her consultation on numerous details of egg cookery; Julia Child, that gracious lady, for her freely given time and advice.

Introduction

My book is about cooking and the love of it. It is for the uninitiated who want to learn two rituals of the kitchen—omelette-making and soufflé-making. It is for the seasoned cook who wants fresh ideas and refined understanding. Finally, it is for the lover of food who enjoys reading cookbooks. To this armchair cook I devote my prose.

With this book the greatest gift that I can give you is confidence in yourself as a cook, a host, a provider. That is the essence of a gracious cook. Because confidence comes from understanding and practice, I urge you to read the introductions to each section. Understanding is the first half of a recipe. If you know the "whys," the "hows" are much simpler.

Practice is the other half of a recipe, and I urge you to try your hand at it. Success in omelette-making is largely the result of the number of eggs that have passed through your pan. Success in soufflé-making is largely the result of the number of whites your whisk has passed through.

With six dozen eggs you will have mastered this book. You can make three omelettes, one frittata, a mousseline omelette for two, egg foo yung for four, a Salzburger nockerl, four hot soufflés of different flavors, a chocolate roulade, two cold soufflés (one to eat and one to freeze), and you will still have enough eggs left over to make two omelettes for breakfast the next morning!

Remember, this is a guidebook, not a rule book; so I encourage you to take all the detours you find interesting. Every recipe in this book can be and often should be varied. Substitute ingredients. Try new seasonings. When you do, it becomes *your* recipe!

The Egg

Consider the egg. Newly laid, it is a gift of nature in naked perfection. Classically shaped, protectively packaged. Nutrition in the raw. Uncracked potential. Handled with care, the earthy egg can be transformed into an offering fit for any table.

Appreciate the practiced hand that performs the miracle. This hand can change the egg from its simple innocence to an appealing omelette or an elusive soufflé. Without the skilled hand, the egg would be left cradled in its nest, never reaching its greatest heights. It would remain an unused gift of the earth's bounty. The skilled hand gives the egg the life that makes it a fit offering to heaven.

Like all miracles, the miracle of egg cookery is not the result of magic, but of love; love that is willing to practice and master basic techniques that complement the egg's natural goodness; the love that comes from a skilled hand.

Omelettes

In the following recipes, this * signifies the point to
which a dish can be prepared ahead of time.

The Omelette

An omelette is honest. It is basic and unadulterated, fashioned from two pure foods of nature: eggs and butter. When so much of our food is processed and packaged, honest food is important to the quality of our lives. Too often, coffee is a tasteless dust, milk is a chalky powder, cheese grows in little green cans, and whipped cream fizzes out of spray containers. Amid all that confusion, an omelette is real.

An omelette is classic. Throughout history, variations of the omelette have nourished the rich and the poor. Often the filling has reflected the diner's purse, but all dine well on an omelette.

An omelette is enough. Its tender goodness, proudly presented, is a meal. You need never apologize for this meal's simplicity. Rather, one should apologize for a meal so encumbered that it is impossible to enjoy the individual foods presented.

An omelette is international. In France, it is called *omelette;* in China, egg *foo yung;* in Italy, *frittata;* in Spain, *tortilla.* Even the Japanese have an omelette called *tamago dashimaki,* which consists of thin layers of eggs cooked in a rectangular pan and then rolled.

An omelette is economical in time, motion and money. You can prepare an omelette faster, with less trouble and less expense than it takes to go to a hasty hamburger house or a cheap chicken chalet. And your body and soul will be greatly blessed by the honest experience.

An omelette is scrambled eggs—but it is not. It starts out similarly, then takes on a shape, texture and finally a flavor distinctly its own. Add a filling to an omelette and you have a surprise package wrapped with eggs. Both the eggs and the filling assume new dimensions from their liaison.

An omelette is easy. All you need to cook an omelette are fresh eggs, a small bowl, a seasoned pan, sweet butter, a table fork, a small spatula, a warm plate—and a practiced hand.

Eggs and Butter

In all cooking, the quality of the raw ingredients greatly determines the outcome of the finished dish. The quality of the eggs and butter in an omelette is particularly important because these ingredients are tasted almost singly.

There are three things to consider when buying eggs—freshness, grade and size—but without freshness, the other two do not matter. If you have hens, you are much blessed. Treat them kindly and gather their labor of love with care and respect. If you do not have hens, cultivate friends who do.

Your grocer's shelves are a far cry from the proud hen's warm nest but a good alternative these days, thanks to the efficiency of American suppliers and the trucking industry. Eggs are reaching your grocer fresher than ever. Some eggs reach the stores within one or two days after they are laid. Check for a dating code on the egg carton for the last day they can be sold. If you find only the date of inspection, be sure it is within 10 days of your purchase.

Grade and size of eggs are two entirely different factors. Grade refers to the quality of the egg and its shell at the time it is packed. Top quality eggs are graded AA, and Grade A eggs are next best. Since eggs are the main ingredient in omelettes, soufflés and their variations, use either Grade AA or Grade A. Eggs are also sorted according to size, into six weight classes: Jumbo, extra large, large, medium, small and peewee. All the egg dishes in this book are based on large eggs that weigh about two ounces each.

The color of the egg shell—brown, white or speckled—has nothing to do with the quality or flavor of the egg inside. It is what the hen eats that determines the flavor of the egg. So cultivate friends who own epicurean hens.

To ensure freshness, refrigerate eggs in their cartons. The cartons will act as a barrier to keep air and odors from seeping into the pores of the shells.

Freshness makes a difference in butter too. If you do not have your own cows and churn, buy the best-quality butter on the shelf. I prefer unsalted (sweet) butter in an omelette, because it allows the flavors to emerge unmasked. But if you prefer, use lightly salted butter.

A Practiced Hand

For eggs and butter to be transformed into an omelette that could win hearts, the cook needs experience. Omelette-making takes time only in the learning, not in the cooking. One evening's practice and a couple of dozen eggs can be an investment in a lifetime of quick, simple meals. With a heavy measure of experience and a healthy dash of confidence, you may rival Madame Poulard, who made her Mont-Saint-Michel restaurant famous for her fluffy omelettes.

Good Equipment

Omelette-making equipment is very personal. I have a special little brown pottery bowl into

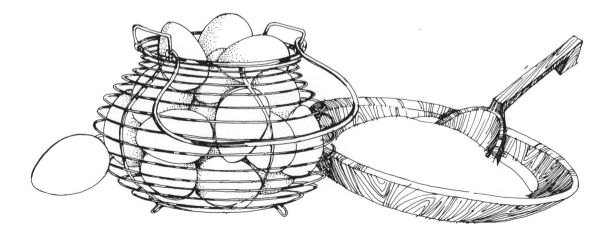

which I crack the egg before lightly breaking the yolks and whites together with a table fork. I always use a table fork, for it seems to stir the eggs better once they are in the pan. The same fork can be used to fold the omelette, but I prefer a small metal spatula with a rounded end. A certain set of plates of a medium size and a sloping rim are always warmed, ready to act as the other half of the pan. Each warm plate catches an omelette as it is turned from the pan, and then holds the food's warmth.

You really do not need to have a special bowl for your omelettes, but your pan should be special. It must have the proper shape, a good weight and the right size. The proper shape for an omelette pan is that of a skillet with outwardly flared or curved sides. This flared shape allows the omelette to roll easily out of the pan onto the plate. It is very difficult to turn an omelette out of a French sauté pan with its straight, vertical sides. Some cooks also prefer a pan with a long handle because the handle does not get too hot.

An omelette pan should be made out of a heavyweight metal that conducts heat evenly and does not develop hot spots. Especially good materials for omelette pans are iron, copper or stainless steel. Heavy cast aluminum is also very good—with or without an anodized surface. Today's technology has also made non-stick surfaces available. These surfaces do not last forever, while a traditional iron omelette pan should. But the advantage of non-stick pans is that they also may be used for cooking foods other than omelettes. This is a plus for someone who does not cook omelettes very frequently because the seasoning of an iron or aluminum pan tends to be less effective when the pan is used only on rare occasions.

THE PAN AND ITS SEASONING

In omelette-making it is the seasoning of the pan's surface that makes the difference. I speak not of seasoning with herbs and spices but of seasoning with oil to prevent eggs from sticking to the pan. It is the same method your grandmother used when seasoning her black cast iron pan. Follow this simple procedure:

When you buy a new omelette pan, clean it to your heart's content! This will be the last time you wash it, so get the washing out of your system. Then dry it thoroughly. To season: Fill the pan with oil, then heat it on a medium-high burner until the oil is hot. Next, turn off the burner but do not remove the pan or the oil may spill on the hot burner. Allow the oil to cool; then remove the pan from the stove and let it sit for six to eight hours or overnight with the oil in it. Then pour out the oil. Finally, wipe the pan with a paper towel and the pan is ready to use. There is nothing wrong with the oil used for seasoning the pan. It has only been heated, so save it to use for future cooking.

After each use of the omelette pan, put a half teaspoon of salt in the pan and scour the inside with the salt and an oiled paper towel. This will remove any food particles and leave an oiled surface. Remember: Do not wash! If the underside of the pan gets dirty, consider it a sign of character.

Wrap the pan in aluminum foil when you store it. An omelette pan should be just that—an omelette pan. Cooking other foods in it requires washing the pan, and washing the pan causes it to lose its seasoning.

Pan Size

Size is important in omelette pans. If you use a pan too small for the number of eggs to be cooked, the resulting omelette will be too thick. A pan that is too large makes an omelette that is thin and dry. A pan that is 8 inches across the top, 5½ inches across the bottom, and 1½ to 2 inches high is perfect for a two- or three-egg omelette. You can even sneak a fourth egg into the pan for a lean and hungry soul. The French omelette, intended for only one person, is generally made with two to three eggs.

Some omelettes are made to be divided and served to several people. If you want to make a larger folded omelette with six to 10 eggs, use a larger pan—9 to 12 inches across the top, 6½ inches across the bottom and 1 to 2 inches high. In this book, recipes for flat omelettes—tortillas, frittatas, and egg foo yung—are designed for serving six, so use a 9- to 12-inch omelette pan.

The Plain Omelette

The following recipe explains the technique for making the traditional folded French omelette. Do not let its length discourage you, for the technique is not difficult. However, the explanation is detailed, so if you have never made an omelette, read the instructions several times before beginning. Assemble your ingredients and have your filling ready. Remember the importance of practice, and if the first omelette does not turn out as well as you might like, eat your mistake—then try again. You will be well-fed and confident in no time.

Though you may feel timid, do not try to make omelettes over a low temperature because low heat makes an omelette stick. High heat causes the eggs to "jump" from the surface of the pan without sticking. So turn up the heat: Your omelettes will be better for it.

The basic ingredients of an omelette are eggs, seasonings and butter. Some cooks add water, milk, cream, sour cream or even crème fraîche to the eggs. All omelettes considered and tasted, I prefer simply eggs, seasonings and butter.

2 to 3 eggs
⅛ teaspoon salt
⅛ teaspoon pepper
1 tablespoon butter

Break the eggs into a small bowl and season with ⅛ teaspoon salt and pepper. Gently stir the egg yolks into the whites with a fork for about 20 strokes. The mixture will not be completely yellow; some whites will still show. Place an empty omelette pan over medium-high to high heat for about 1 minute (15 to 30 seconds for succeeding omelettes). Spear 1 tablespoon of butter with the prongs of the fork. Touch the butter to the bottom of the pan. If the butter sizzles, drop the butter pat in immediately. If the butter does not sizzle, allow the pan to heat a few more seconds and test again. When the butter sizzles, drop in the butter pat. Lift the pan from the burner and swirl the butter around so that it coats the bottom and sides of the pan.

When the butter has melted, place the pan on the burner and quickly pour in the eggs. Immediately begin stirring the eggs with a fork, keeping the fork's tines parallel to the bottom of the pan. Use large circular motions, spreading the eggs over the bottom of the pan. After about 30 seconds the eggs will begin to get creamy and thick, and small holes will appear as the fork is passing through the mass of egg. Spread any liquid portion of the eggs into the holes with the fork to form a soft, solid bed of eggs. The eggs will look cooked around the edges and will pull away from the pan, but the center should still be moist.

If the omelette is to be filled, place the filling in a strip across the omelette's center. Lift the pan handle up so that the far side of the pan is lower than the handle side. With a fork or small spatula, lift the unfilled portion of the omelette

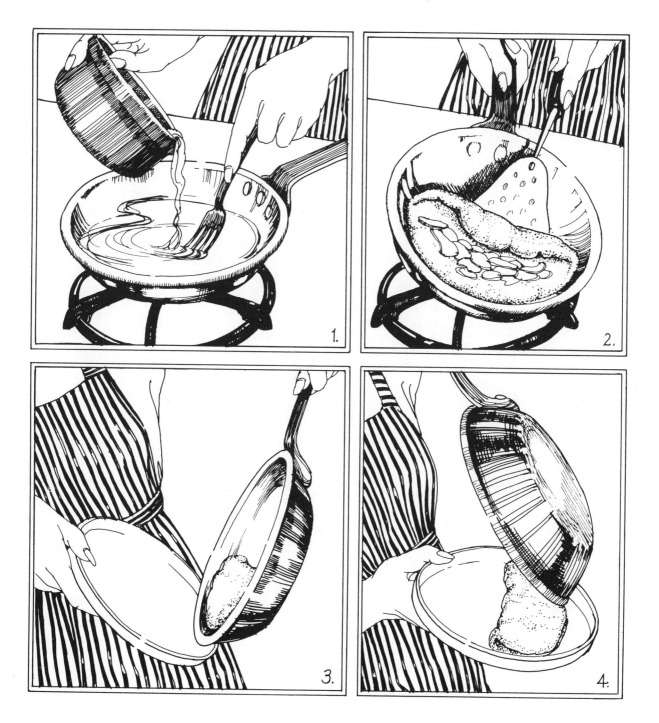

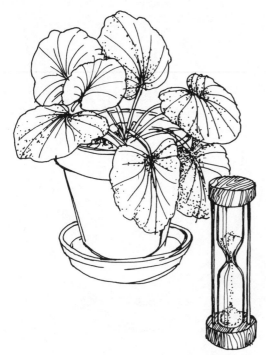

and let it fall over the filling. The portion that is folded over should be a little more than a third of the omelette.

The portion of the omelette that is now on the bottom is still slightly exposed. Shake the pan to loosen the omelette, slide it to the center of the pan and allow the omelette to brown slightly.

Grasp the handle of the omelette pan from underneath. Your palm should be on the bottom, fingers on top and thumb pointing away from the pan. Raise the handle up and tilt the pan down, allowing the omelette to slide to the far edge. Hold a warm plate vertically and tilt the pan, placing the far edge of the pan inside the rim of the plate. Gradually turn the pan upside down toward the plate and allow the omelette to roll onto the plate, tucking the far edge of the omelette under as it rolls. The top of the omelette is the middle third; the edges and seam are tucked underneath. This whole process should take about a minute. Garnish if you wish, and serve.

Herb Omelette

To make an Herb Omelette, add 1 tablespoon of fresh, chopped herb or 1 teaspoon of dried herb to the eggs before cooking. The Herb Omelette may be served as is, or with any of the complementary savory fillings.

OMELETTES FOR A CAST OF THOUSANDS

A world-record omelette was once made of 5,600 eggs! It weighed 1,234 pounds and was cooked in a 6-by-7-foot omelette pan. Though you probably do not have omelettes of this magnitude in mind, larger omelettes do require a larger pan and a little more cooking time—and often the resulting omelette may not be as creamy and evenly cooked as a smaller one.

However, making individual omelettes can be time-consuming when you are cooking for a large group or party. To speed up the process, break all the eggs into a bowl, season them and then ladle the mixture out for each omelette. Have an assortment of fillings ready so that each guest may choose his own. And if you must hold the omelettes for a few minutes, use a warming tray or warming oven.

The following pages are full of ideas for omelette fillings. However, it is presumptuous of me to make suggestions for fillings, because what you put in an omelette should be between you and your refrigerator. An omelette is an ingenious disguise for last night's leftovers. Reclaim an abandoned zucchini, the remnants of a bunch of scallions and a few lonely mushrooms, cook them in butter, and you have a filling fit for anyone's table.

Whatever ingredients you choose, be sure that they are as cooked as you want them to be before you put them in the omelette. Also be sure that the fillings are hot, if they need to be. Canned foods will need to be heated, of course.

The following are filling ideas for a two- or three-egg omelette.

- ½ cup grated cheese—the stronger the cheese, the more flavorful the omelette.
- Cheese and nuts. Example: ¼ cup crumbled blue cheese and 2 tablespoons sunflower seeds.
- ½ cup ratatouille.
- ¼ cup each of chopped avocado and chopped tomato.
- ½ cup creamed spinach.
- ½ cup chopped tomato with ½ cup of guacamole topping.
- Fill omelette with 1 tablespoon of caviar and top with 1 tablespoon sour cream.

Plain Savory Omelette Fillings

All fillings in this section are based on two- or three-egg plain, savory omelettes unless otherwise stated. Omelettes are splendid fare for dining alone or with others. All the recipes for fillings can be doubled, tripled or halved to suit the number of diners.

Your life will be greatly diminished if you eat omelettes only for breakfast or brunch. Lunch and light suppers are especially convenient moments to enjoy an omelette. Simply add a salad, an honest loaf of bread and a glass of Fumé Blanc, Chablis, Beaujolais, Zinfandel or whatever your pleasure. For heartier evening fare, serve an omelette as a first course. Thereafter, the sky is the limit. Just stay away from egg-based sauces and desserts.

Mushroom Omelette

For 2 omelettes

1½ tablespoons butter
1 whole scallion, chopped
1 cup fresh mushrooms, sliced
2 tablespoons chopped fresh
    tarragon, dill weed or lemon
    thyme, or 2 teaspoons dried of
    each herb

Melt the butter over medium-high heat. Add the scallion and cook about 1 minute. Cook the mushrooms for 2 minutes. Set aside.*

For each omelette, add 1 tablespoon of fresh herbs to the egg mixture, as you add seasonings. Reserve the remaining tablespoon for a garnish.

Proceed with making the omelettes. When each is ready to fill, spoon half of the mushroom mixture into it. Fold the omelette, turn onto a plate, garnish each with half of the remaining chopped herbs, and serve hot.

NOTE: Do not soak mushrooms in water to clean them, or they will absorb the liquid and become waterlogged. Simply wipe them with a damp paper towel.

Dilled Zucchini Omelette

For 4 omelettes

3 tablespoons butter
2 cups grated or julienned zucchini
1 teaspoon dill weed
¼ teaspoon salt

Melt 3 tablespoons of butter in a small skillet. Add the prepared zucchini and sprinkle with dill weed and salt. Toss over medium-high heat for 3 minutes, until cooked but still slightly crunchy.*

Fill each omelette with a quarter of the zucchini mixture. Fold the omelette, turn onto plate and serve hot.

Omelette Provençale

For 4 omelettes

2 tablespoons butter
1 medium-size onion, thinly sliced
1 clove garlic, minced
2 tomatoes, peeled, seeded and chopped
3 tablespoons fresh parsley, or
    2 teaspoons dried
3 tablespoons fresh basil, or
    2 teaspoons dried
⅛ teaspoon salt
⅛ teaspoon pepper

Melt the butter in a small saucepan. Cook the onion in butter until soft. Do not brown. Add garlic, tomato, 2 tablespoons each of chopped parsley and basil, and ⅛ teaspoon each of salt and pepper. Cook over medium heat for about 2 minutes.*

When each omelette is ready to fill, spoon a quarter of the tomato mixture into it. Fold the omelette and turn onto plate. Garnish each omelette with a mixture of the remaining herbs. Serve hot.

Smoked Turkey Omelette

For 2 omelettes

2 tablespoons butter
1 scallion, whites and tops, chopped
½ cup julienned smoked turkey
½ cup sliced fresh mushrooms
⅛ teaspoon salt
1 tablespoon chopped fresh parsley,
    to garnish

Melt the butter in a small skillet. Cook the chopped scallions for 2 minutes over medium-high heat. Add the julienned turkey, mushrooms and salt.* Cook for about 2 minutes or until hot.

When each omelette is ready to fill, place half of the mixture in it. Fold and turn onto a plate. Garnish each omelette with half of the chopped parsley.

Asparagus and Tarragon Omelette

For 2 omelettes

1 teaspoon butter
8 spears cooked asparagus
1 tablespoon chopped fresh
    tarragon, or 1 teaspoon dried

Melt the butter over medium-high heat. Add asparagus spears and sprinkle with the tarragon. Toss until the asparagus is heated through.

When each omelette is ready to fill, place half of the asparagus in it. Fold and turn onto a plate. Serve hot.

NOTE: This is a delicious use of leftover asparagus or broccoli.

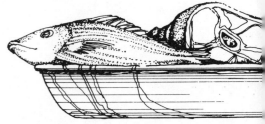

Sardine and Tarragon Omelette

For 4 omelettes

1 tablespoon Dijon mustard
3¾-ounce can skinless and boneless
   sardines, drained
1 tablespoon chopped fresh
   tarragon, or 1 teaspoon dried
1 tablespoon minced scallions
2 tablespoons chopped fresh parsley
   or tarragon, to garnish

Combine the first 4 ingredients thoroughly.*

When each omelette is ready to fill, spoon a quarter of the mixture into it. Fold the omelette and turn onto a plate. Garnish each with 1½ teaspoons of herbs and serve hot.

NOTE: When substituting dried herbs for fresh herbs, use one-third the amount of the fresh herbs.

Ham, Mushroom and Cheese Omelette

For 2 omelettes

1 tablespoon butter
1 scallion, whites and tops, chopped
½ cup cooked ham, cut in ½-inch
   squares or julienne strips
½ cup fresh mushrooms, sliced
2 tablespoons freshly grated
   Parmesan cheese

Melt the butter in a small skillet. Cook the scallions for 2 minutes over medium-high heat. Add ham and mushrooms. Cook about 2 minutes until hot.*

When the omelette is ready to fill, place half the ham mixture in each omelette. Sprinkle 1 tablespoon of Parmesan cheese on top of the ham. Fold the omelette, turn onto a plate, and serve hot.

Avocado, Artichoke Heart and Tomato Omelette

For 4 omelettes

1 medium-size tomato, peeled,
   seeded and cubed
1 avocado (best slightly firm),
   peeled and cubed
4 ounces artichoke hearts (about
   4 or 5), quartered
1 tablespoon fresh basil or chervil

Stir all ingredients together in a bowl. Reserve about ¾ cup to use as a garnish. Divide the remainder into 4 portions and spoon into the omelettes when they are ready for filling. Then fold the omelettes. Allow a little extra time for the filling to warm. Turn onto a plate, garnish with reserved filling, and serve hot.

NOTE: If you must use dried basil or chervil, use 1 teaspoon each and add to eggs instead of filling.

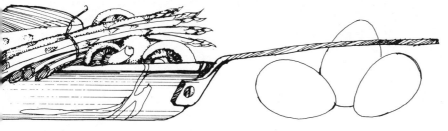

Smoked Oyster Omelette with Horseradish Sauce

For 4 omelettes

3 tablespoons fresh horseradish, or prepared horseradish
½ cup sour cream
⅛ teaspoon salt
3- to 4-ounce can smoked oysters, drained
¼ cup chopped fresh chives, to garnish

Mix the horseradish, sour cream and salt together to make a sauce.*

When each omelette is ready to fill, place a quarter of the oysters in it. Fold and turn onto plate. Garnish each omelette with 1 tablespoon of the chopped chives and serve 2 tablespoons of horseradish sauce on the side.

Shrimp and Gruyère Omelette

For 4 omelettes

1 tablespoon butter
2 scallions, whites and tops, chopped
1 cup shrimp, cooked, peeled and chopped
3 tablespoons chopped parsley
1 cup Gruyère cheese

Melt the butter in a saucepan over medium-high heat. Add the scallions and cook until soft but not browned. Add the shrimp, sprinkle with 1 tablespoon of the parsley and cook over medium heat until heated through, about 1 minute.*

When each omelette is ready to fill, place ¼ cup shrimp and ¼ cup Gruyère cheese in it, fold and turn onto a plate. Garnish each omelette with ½ tablespoon of the remaining parsley.

Virginia Ham Omelette

For 1 omelette

1 tablespoon ground Smithfield or country ham
¼ cup New York State sharp cheese, grated

When the omelette is ready to fill, sprinkle it with the ham. Sprinkle the grated cheese on top of the ham, fold the omelette, turn onto a plate and serve hot.

NOTE: This is a good use for the hard end of a country ham. Just grind the ham in a food processor or blender until it has a finely chopped consistency.

The Plain Sweet Omelette

To make only the savory omelettes, and never the sweet, is to use merely half of the plain omelette's possibilities. The plain sweet omelette, so often the answer to a last-minute dessert or late-night snack, can be served with or without a filling.

To make a sweet omelette, substitute two teaspoons of sugar for the salt in a two- to three-egg omelette. For an unfilled sweet omelette, sprinkle superfine sugar over the top after folding and glaze under the broiler.

Jam or Jelly Omelette

For the simplest filling, use two tablespoons of your favorite jelly, jam or fruit preserves. Decorate the finished omelette with a dusting of powdered sugar.

Mixed Fruit with Crème Pâtissière

For 6 sweet omelettes

3 small apples, peeled, cored and cut
    into thin wedges
2 pears, peeled, cored and cut into
    thin wedges
2 tablespoons sugar
1 tablespoon butter
Zest of 1 orange
¼ cup orange juice
¼ cup rum
½ cup seedless raisins
2 cups Crème Pâtissière

CRÈME PÂTISSIÈRE

5 egg yolks
¾ cup sugar
½ cup flour, sifted
2 cups milk
1 vanilla bean or ½ teaspoon vanilla
    extract or 2 tablespoons liqueur
⅛ teaspoon salt

Combine the fruit, sugar, butter, zest, orange juice, rum and raisins in a saucepan. Simmer about 15 minutes, or until cooked but not too soft.*

When each omelette is ready to fill, spoon one-sixth of the fruit mixture into it. Fold and turn onto a plate. Top each omelette with a third of a cup of the warm Crème Pâtissière and serve.

NOTE: The zest of an orange is the colored part of the citrus rind. The zest adds flavor but—unlike the white—leaves no bitter aftertaste.

Makes about 2 cups

Beat the yolks in a bowl, gradually adding the sugar. When the mixture is very pale and light, add the flour. Beat until the mixture is just smooth.

Heat the milk in a saucepan with a 1-inch piece of vanilla bean or other flavoring until very warm. Then remove the vanilla bean. Slowly pour the flavored milk into the egg mixture, whisking constantly. Add the salt. Transfer to a saucepan and cook over medium-high heat. Whisk constantly until the sauce comes just to a boil. Reduce heat and cook for 2 or 3 minutes, stirring constantly.

NOTE: Be sure to run the whisk around the "corners" of the saucepan while whisking, so the sauce will not scorch in these areas.

Banana Apricot Omelette

For 4 sweet omelettes

2 bananas, sliced
1 tablespoon brown sugar
1 tablespoon sweet vermouth
3 tablespoons apricot preserves
3 tablespoons toasted slivered
   almonds
1 tablespoon powdered sugar, to
   decorate

Combine the bananas, brown sugar, sweet vermouth and apricot preserves in a small bowl.

When each sweet omelette is ready to fill, spoon in a quarter of the fruit filling. Then sprinkle 1 teaspoon toasted almonds on top of the filling. Fold the omelette and turn onto a plate. Dust each omelette lightly with powdered sugar and decorate each with about 1 teaspoon of almonds. Serve immediately.

Green Grape Omelette

For 2 sweet omelettes

½ cup seedless grapes, halved
2 teaspoons brown sugar
2 tablespoons sour cream or yogurt,
   to decorate
½ teaspoon ground cinnamon, to
   decorate

Stir the grapes and brown sugar together.*

When each sweet omelette is ready to fill, spoon half of the grape mixture into it. Fold and turn onto a plate. Decorate each omelette with 1 tablespoon sour cream and sprinkle with ¼ teaspoon cinnamon.

NOTE: Fresh sliced strawberries, sliced bananas or sliced peaches can be substituted for the green grapes.

Strawberry with Mint Omelette

For 4 sweet omelettes

1 pint fresh strawberries, sliced
1 teaspoon chopped fresh mint
1 tablespoon powdered sugar to
  decorate

Combine the strawberries and mint in a small bowl.*

When each sweet omelette is ready to fill, spoon ½ cup of the strawberry mixture into it. Fold the omelette, turn onto a plate, and dust lightly with powdered sugar. Serve immediately.

NOTE: Fresh sliced peaches or blueberries are a good substitute for the strawberries.

Honey Omelette

For 1 omelette

There are several legends about the origins of the omelette. A credible theory is that the word "omelette" derives from the Latin ova mellita, *or "honeyed eggs." My honey omelette recipe, inspired by this Roman favorite, substitutes honey for the sugar of a sweet omelette.*

2 eggs
1 tablespoon honey
1 tablespoon finely chopped pecans,
  walnuts or pine nuts
1 teaspoon powdered sugar, to
  decorate

Break the eggs into a small bowl and add the honey. Beat to incorporate the 2 mixtures—about 20 times. Add no other seasonings.

Make the omelette according to the basic omelette recipe.

When ready to fill, sprinkle the omelette with chopped nuts. Fold and turn out onto a plate. Using a sieve, dust with powdered sugar and serve.

NOTE: For an interesting variation, fill this honey omelette with 1 ounce grated Swiss cheese and 1 tablespoon raisins.

Flat Omelettes: Tortillas, Frittatas and Egg Foo Yung

The Spanish, Italians and Chinese take different approaches to cooking omelettes. The fillings are cooked in the same pan as the eggs, and the omelette is flat, not folded. Instead of butter, the Spanish tortilla and the Italian frittata are cooked in their native olive oil. The Chinese use peanut oil in their omelettes.

The Spanish Tortilla

Years ago, when I spent a summer in Spain, rarely a week passed without the pleasure of a *tortilla de patata* for a late-night repast with the family I was visiting. (The Spanish tortilla is a flat omelette, not the cornmeal-breadlike tortilla of Mexico.)

Maria, who did the cooking, always began with sizzling olive oil, a clove of garlic and thinly sliced white potatoes. Most often, those were the only ingredients for the tortilla. Other evenings, she added chopped onions, or other chopped vegetables or chorizo, the Spanish sausage.

As the potatoes cooked in the hot oil and garlic, Maria gently combined the yolks and whites with a fork. Then she poured the eggs into the omelette pan with the tender potatoes. She drew the egg mixture across the pan with a spatula until large curds of cooked egg formed. Maria smoothed the top of the tortilla and, with a spatula, loosened the omelette from the pan. Then she inverted it onto a plate and slid the tortilla back in to cook the other side for a minute. She served it to us in pie-shaped wedges accompanied by steaming soup and a salad. *¡Qué delicioso!*

Once, for a special birthday picnic held on a mountain overlooking Burgos, Maria tucked her tortilla into a round loaf of bread. It looked like a big sandwich and was delicious when cut and served cold in pie-shaped wedges. Cold tortilla is very flavorful because of the olive oil and garlic, especially when accompanied by a gazpacho salad, a local goat cheese, a good Spanish Rioja and a rich *torta* for a birthday cake.

The type of pan you use for cooking tortillas and frittatas is very important. A large pan, of the same shape as the plain French omelette pan, is usually used. Since the filling is cooked in the same pan as the eggs, sticking often occurs. A well-seasoned iron or non-stick surfaced pan will solve this problem. After each use, clean the iron pan by rubbing oil and salt into the surface, then wipe the pan and put it away slightly oiled.

A tortilla is too heavy to flip, so I use Maria's method of sliding the tortilla out onto a plate. First, cover the pan with a flat plate and, while holding the plate and pan together, invert them and the tortilla will then fall out onto the plate. Then slide the tortilla back into the pan, cooked side up, and brown the uncooked side.

If you are nervous about taking the tortilla out of the pan, slip the tortilla under the broiler to cook the top. If you use an attractive ovenproof pan, you can serve the tortilla hot from the pan.

Italian Frittata

The frittata, the Italian omelette, is flat, like the Spanish omelette. The chief difference between the two omelettes is not in the technique, but in the ingredients. Spanish ingredients are used in the tortilla and Italian ingredients are used in the frittata. The Italians frequently cook their fillings, then add the filling to the eggs. The entire mixture is then poured back into the same pan to cook. (The Spanish pour the eggs into the pan, on top of the cooked filling.) Use either method when making the tortilla or the frittata.

Egg Foo Yung

The Chinese also have an omelette, called egg foo yung. Classic egg foo yung is an airy soufflé puffed with egg whites and flavored with pieces of chicken. The egg foo yung we are more familiar with is a flat egg pie filled with Chinese ingredients. Here again, like the tortilla and frittata, the filling is cooked with the eggs and the omelette is served flat.

The Chinese omelette, however, has some differences. The proportion of eggs to filling is not as large as the Spanish and Italian versions, and peanut oil is used instead of olive oil. Egg foo yung is also smaller than these other omelettes. Small ladles of egg mixtures are cooked in hot oil so that the omelettes cook to about the diameter of a hamburger.

Naturally, Chinese ingredients are used in the filling. The Chinese love crisp vegetables, so they shred their fillings (cut them in shapes which range from julienne strips to thin threads) and cook the fillings *only* until they are heated. Though egg foo yung is usually pan-fried, it can be deep-fried as well. Frequently, egg foo yung is served with a sauce.

Egg foo yung can be cooked in a wok or a skillet—no special omelette pan is needed. When using a wok, you need only one tablespoon of oil. Because of the wok's shape, oil concentrates in the bottom and less is needed.

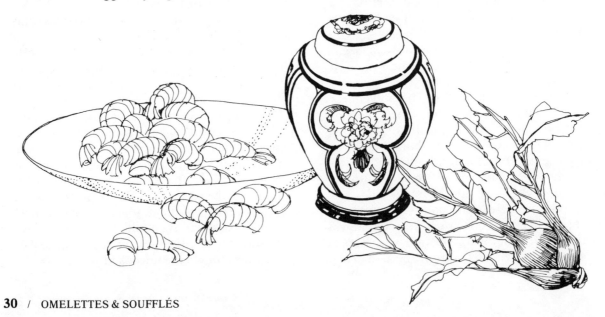

Potato Tortilla

2 tablespoons olive oil
1 large baking potato, peeled,
  halved and sliced into half-moons
  about ⅛ inch thick
½ teaspoon salt
2 cloves garlic, minced
6-8 eggs
¼ teaspoon salt
⅛ teaspoon pepper

Heat the olive oil in a heavy 9- to 10-inch omelette pan over medium-high temperature for 2 minutes. Add the potatoes and sprinkle with ½ teaspoon salt. The potatoes should sizzle but not brown when added to the oil. Turn the potatoes to coat them well with the oil, and cook over medium heat for about 5 minutes. Turn heat to low. Add the garlic and continue to cook, tossing frequently for about 5 more minutes. When done, the potatoes should be translucent. Some potatoes may be faintly browning around the edges at this stage.*

Meanwhile, break the eggs into a bowl. Season with ¼ teaspoon salt and ⅛ teaspoon pepper. Barely blend the egg yolks into the whites with a fork.

When the potatoes are ready, turn the heat to high. Pour in the eggs and combine. As the mixture cooks, pull a spatula through it along the bottom of the pan, turning clumps of the mixture over as it cooks. After about 2 to 3 minutes, when the mixture begins to thicken, pat down the top of the omelette to smooth it. When the omelette moves together as a mass, it is ready to turn. It should be firm on the bottom but not on the top.

To loosen the omelette from the pan, slide a spatula under the eggs and go all the way around the omelette. Then, with the spatula under the eggs, go to the center of the pan, loosening the center of the omelette. Remove the spatula, then cover the pan with a flat plate and while holding the plate and pan together, invert them so that the omelette falls onto the plate. Remove the pan and turn it upright again. Carefully slide the omelette, cooked side up, back into the pan. Cook for 1 to 2 more minutes to brown the other side and serve immediately. Slice into wedges for serving.

Variations on the Potato Tortilla

For the following omelettes, add the suggested ingredients to the Potato Tortilla at the point when the garlic is added.

POTATO AND ONION TORTILLA

1 medium-size onion, peeled, halved
   and thinly sliced (about ¾ cup)

POTATO AND CHORIZO TORTILLA

1 chorizo, sliced into ¼-inch rounds

LAMB TORTILLA

1 leek, chopped (about ½ cup)
½ pound uncooked ground lamb
2 teaspoons each of chopped fresh
   oregano and rosemary

    For this tortilla, reduce to ½ cup the quantity of potato slices in the Potato Tortilla. Add the leek, ground lamb and herbs at the point when the garlic is added.

VEGETABLE TORTILLA

1 medium-size onion, peeled, halved
   and thinly sliced
½ medium-size green pepper,
   seeded and chopped (about ½ cup)
1 tablespoon each of chopped fresh
   oregano, chives and basil
1 medium-size tomato, peeled,
   seeded and chopped (about ¾ cup)

For this tortilla, you should reduce the quantity of potato in the Potato Tortilla to 1 cup. Add the onion and the pepper at the point when the garlic is added and the herbs and chopped tomato just before adding the eggs.

Eggplant Frittata

Makes a 9- to 10-inch frittata that serves 2 to 4

3 tablespoons olive oil
1 clove of garlic, minced
¼ cup chopped onion
2 cups cubed eggplant (½-inch
   cubes)
1 large tomato, peeled, seeded and
   chopped (about 1 cup)
½ teaspoon salt
6 eggs
¼ teaspoon salt
⅛ teaspoon pepper

Heat 2 tablespoons of the olive oil in a heavy 9- to 10-inch omelette pan over medium-high heat. Add garlic and onion, and cook for 2 minutes. Add the eggplant and cook for 3 minutes, tossing occasionally. Add the tomato and ½ teaspoon salt. Remove from heat and reserve to add to the eggs.*

Break the eggs into a bowl. Season with ¼ teaspoon salt and ⅛ teaspoon pepper. Barely blend the egg yolks into the whites with a fork. Stir the vegetable mixture into the eggs and combine.

Place the omelette pan over high heat. Add the remaining tablespoon of olive oil to the pan. Pour the egg mixture into the pan. As the mixture cooks, pull a spatula through it along the bottom of the pan, turning clumps of the mixture over as it cooks. After 2 to 3 minutes, when the mixture begins to thicken, pat down the top of the omelette to smooth it. When the omelette moves together as a mass, it is ready to turn. It should be firm on the bottom but not on the top.

To loosen the omelette from the pan, slide a spatula under the eggs and go all the way around the omelette. Then, with the spatula under the eggs, go to the center of the pan, loosening the center of the omelette. Remove the spatula and cover the pan with a flat plate. While holding the plate and pan together, invert them so that the omelette falls onto the plate. Remove the pan and turn it upright again. Carefully slide the omelette, cooked side up, back into the pan. Cook for 1 to 2 more minutes to brown the other side. Slide onto plate and serve immediately. Slice into wedges for serving.

Variations on the Eggplant Frittata

In the following recipes, you may substitute the ingredients listed for the eggplant and the tomato in the Eggplant Frittata, at the points indicated.

ZUCCHINI AND PARMESAN FRITTATA

**2 cups grated zucchini, instead of
the eggplant and tomato
¼ cup grated Parmesan cheese**

Follow the original recipe until the point at which you add the vegetable mixture to the eggs. Then also stir in the Parmesan cheese and proceed to make the frittata.

BROCCOLI FRITTATA

**2 cups fresh broccoli florets instead
of the onion, eggplant and tomato
½ cup dry white wine**

Follow the original recipe until the broccoli is well coated with oil. Then add the white wine to the pan and simmer for 5 minutes, or until the liquid has evaporated. Add the broccoli and garlic mixture to the eggs and proceed to make the frittata.

RICE AND FETA CHEESE FRITTATA

**FILLING (this replaces entire
eggplant filling):
2 tablespoons oil
1 clove of garlic, chopped
1 cup feta cheese, crumbled
1 cup cooked rice**

Heat the oil over medium-high heat in a heavy omelette pan. Add the chopped garlic and cook for about 1 minute. Combine with the crumbled cheese and rice. Add the mixture to the eggs and proceed to make the frittata.

Chicken and Tree Ear Egg Foo Yung

Makes 8 small omelettes to serve 4

½ cup dried tree ears or Chinese
  mushrooms
1 cup water
3 tablespoons peanut oil
1 scallion, white and top, cut into
  strips
1 cup shredded cooked chicken
½ cup bean sprouts
2 tablespoons sherry
1 tablespoon soy sauce
4 eggs
¼ teaspoon salt

Soak the tree ears in water for 10 minutes, then drain.

Heat 1 tablespoon of the oil in a small skillet. Add the scallions and stir-fry for 1 minute. Add the chicken, tree ears, bean sprouts, sherry and soy sauce, and cook for 1 minute, stirring to combine flavors. Set aside.*

Break the eggs into a small bowl. Season with ¼ teaspoon salt. Gently blend the egg yolks into the whites with a fork for about 15 strokes. Add the chicken mixture to the eggs and combine.

Heat the remaining 2 tablespoons of oil in a medium-sized skillet or wok. Ladle ¼ cup of the egg mixture into the oil and allow it to cook on one side for 30 seconds to 1 minute, or until brown and set. Turn the omelette and allow it to cook on the other side for 30 seconds to 1 minute. Remove the omelette from the pan with a spatula. Repeat the process with the remainder of the mixture, cooking 1 omelette at a time.

NOTE: To stir-fry is to stir foods constantly and quickly in hot oil. This rapid cooking seals in the flavor and moisture of the foods as well as their vitamins.

Pork and Cabbage Egg Foo Yung
Makes 8 small omelettes to serve 4

1 cup thin strips of cooked pork
1 teaspoon 5-spice powder
1 tablespoon soy sauce
¼ cup sliced water chestnuts
1 cup shredded Chinese cabbage
4 eggs
¼ teaspoon salt
2 tablespoons peanut oil

Mix together the pork, 5-spice powder, soy sauce, water chestnuts and Chinese cabbage in a bowl. Set aside.*

Break the eggs into a small bowl. Season with ¼ teaspoon salt. Gently blend the egg yolks into the whites with a fork for about 15 strokes. Add the pork mixture to the eggs and combine.

Heat the oil in a medium-sized skillet or wok. Ladle ¼ cup of the egg mixture into the oil and allow it to cook on one side for 30 seconds to 1 minute, until brown and set. Turn the omelette and allow it to cook on the other side for 30 seconds to 1 minute. Remove the omelette from the pan with a spatula. Repeat the process with the remainder of the mixture, cooking 1 omelette at a time.

NOTE: A delicious variation of this recipe would be to substitute barbecued pork.

Shrimp and Snow Peas Egg Foo Yung
Makes 8 small omelettes to serve 4

3 tablespoons peanut oil
2 scallions, whites and tops, cut in
    julienne strips
1 tablespoon julienned fresh ginger
1 cup snow peas, cut in half
    diagonally
¾ pound shrimp, peeled and
    chopped (approximately 1 cup)
1 tablespoon soy sauce
4 eggs
¼ teaspoon salt

Heat 1 tablespoon of the oil in a small skillet. Add the scallions and ginger and stir-fry for 1 minute. Add the snow peas and stir-fry for 1 minute. Add the shrimp and stir-fry for 1 minute. Stir in 1 tablespoon of soy sauce. Set aside.*

Break the eggs into a small bowl. Season with ¼ teaspoon salt. Gently blend the egg yolks into the whites with a fork for about 15 strokes. Add the shrimp mixture to the eggs and combine.

Heat the remaining 2 tablespoons of oil in a medium-sized skillet or wok. Ladle ¼ cup of the egg mixture into the oil and allow it to cook on one side for 30 seconds to 1 minute, until brown and set. Turn the omelette and allow it to cook on the other side for 30 seconds to 1 minute. Remove the omelette from the pan with a spatula. Repeat the process with the remainder of the mixture, cooking 1 omelette at a time.

Airy Omelettes

Yolks and whites beaten separately, then gently folded together, create the light texture of the mousseline omelette, the omelette soufflé and the Salzburger nockerl. For a detailed explanation of techniques, see the sections that follow.

The Separated Egg

The whole egg, lightly beaten and quickly cooked, creates the creamy omelette. The separated egg and the magic of the whisk create the airy omelettes and soufflés. The light texture of the mousseline omelette, the omelette soufflé, the Salzburger nockerl, the roulade and the soufflé itself is the result of the yolks and whites being separated, well beaten and then folded together again.

Egg whites and air are the secret. When air is properly beaten into the egg whites, they are no longer merely a liquid but a moist airy mound ready to puff up when heated. The only pieces of equipment needed to create this mound of egg whites and air are a copper bowl, a whisk and a strong arm; or, a good electric mixer and a bit of cream of tartar.

Egg whites rise to their greatest heights in a copper bowl because the albumen in the whites reacts chemically to the acidity of the unlined copper. This reaction stabilizes the whites and allows them to hold the air that is beaten into them. Properly beaten egg whites expand to seven times their original volume.

You can also beat egg whites with an electric mixer, but they rise to only five or six times their original volume. While hand-beating in a copper bowl is best, a mixer-made soufflé is still very good. So if you would rather save your arm for tennis, rely on your mixer.

When using a mixer, you need to add cream of tartar as an acid stabilizer to keep the whites from deflating. As you beat the whites and they begin to foam, add ¼ teaspoon cream of tartar for every four egg whites and ⅛ teaspoon salt to flavor the whites (even for sweet mixtures). Cream of tartar is unnecessary in a copper bowl.

Whatever bowl you use, be sure that it is very clean. Egg whites will not beat to the proper volume if there is a trace of grease in the bowl. Clean the inside of your copper bowl by sprinkling it with a little salt and rubbing the interior with a lemon half. The abrasive salt and acidic juice cut any oil or grease that may have collected from the air of the kitchen. Like traces of grease in the bowl, a trace of egg yolk in the egg whites will also prevent the whites from achieving the proper volume.

Whisking the Whites in a Copper Bowl

A copper bowl must be large enough for the quantity of eggs to be beaten. A bowl 10 inches in diameter is an adequate size for most home cooking. A bowl larger than 12 inches is cumbersome. And if you do not have a copper bowl, use any glass or metal bowl—except aluminum. Aluminum tends to make the egg whites gray.

A balloon whisk is the best utensil for beating egg whites in any bowl. It is called a balloon whisk because it has a bulbous, balloon-like shape that allows more space for air among the flexible wires—air that will be whisked into the whites.

According to tradition, and in the view of many of the world's outstanding cooks, eggs must be kept at room temperature before they are beaten. This way, the volume achieved is said to be greater.

I feel that freshness rather than the temperature has more to do with an egg white's (or yolk's) ability to expand. I would rather whisk a cold, fresh egg than an older egg at room temperature. For this reason, use eggs from the most recently purchased carton or—better still—chase a chicken. Even if the eggs are cold, my strong arm seems able to whisk them to a volume comparable to that of room-temperature eggs.

To begin whisking, break up the egg whites by rolling the whisk's handle between the palms of your hands so that the whisk's wires agitate the egg whites. Stop after about 30 seconds. Add ⅛ teaspoon salt, so that the egg whites will not be bland—even if you are going to use them in a sweet dish.

Then begin moving the whisk in a circular motion. Move the whisk down into the whites and up into the air in a circle, pulling the whites into the air and back into the bowl. The top half of the circle will be in the air above the bowl and the bottom half of the circle will be down in the whites. You will almost form a tunnel as the whites move from the bowl into the air and back again. At first, the whites will be liquid and sloshy—then frothy. After about two minutes of beating, soft peaks will appear, although the whites are still very loose. (This is called the "soft-peak" stage.) Continue whisking until the whites begin to tighten up and move in a mass, then whisk about 30 seconds more. When you lift your whisk from the whites, they should now form stiff peaks. (This is called the "stiff-peak" stage.) Do not beat the egg whites until they are dry. They should form peaks but still be moist.

At the stiff-peak stage you should be able to turn the bowl over and the egg whites will keep their shape and stay in the bowl, as if by magic. Though I have confidence in this trick, I suggest that you do not perform it over your Oriental rug.

Once you begin whisking, do not stop—not even to visit with a dear friend—because the egg whites will lose some of their breath and begin to weep for you.

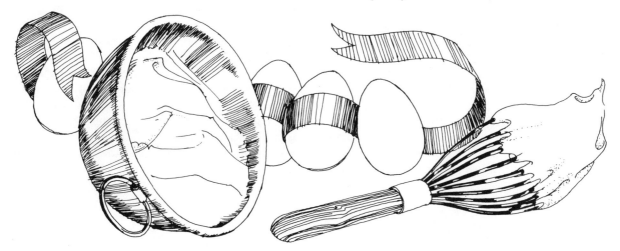

The Other Half of the Egg

After egg whites are beaten, they are often combined with beaten egg yolks. Many recipes will direct you to beat the yolks until they are thick and "mousse-like." The term "mousse-like" refers to that point when the mixture becomes very thick and creamy like a mousse, with the yolks a pale yellow.

To test if the yolks are mousse-like, lift your whisk or beater out of the mixture. A slow stream of the yolks will drip back into the bowl. This slowly dripping mixture sometimes is called a slowly dissolving ribbon. Now dip your beater back into the yolks. Lift it and, with the dissolving ribbon, write the letter "M" on the surface of the yolks. If you can see the first up-stroke of the "M" when you have finished writing the last down-stroke of the "M," the mixture is thick and mousse-like.

Folding

Use a wire whisk when it is time to get the separated egg back together again—*not* a rubber spatula. A whisk holds and even adds air to the whites, while a rubber spatula can knock the air out of the beaten egg white.

To combine the beaten egg whites with the beaten yolks, or any heavier mixture, whisk roughly one cup of whites into the mixture to lighten it. Then pour the mixture down the inside edge of the egg-white bowl. (If the bowl containing the yolks or heavier sauce is the same or larger size than the bowl with the whites, add the egg whites to the yolk bowl. Usually, though, this is not the case.) Fold the whites into the mixture by placing your whisk on the far side of the bowl and pulling the whisk downward, through the center of the mixture, along the bottom of

the bowl and up the side near you. While folding with one hand, use the other hand to turn the bowl a quarter turn, as you pull the whisk up and out. (Do not rap your whisk on the lip of the bowl to shake the mixture from the whisk, for you will be knocking the air out of the eggs!)

Fold until the two mixtures are just combined. Overmixing can undo all the work you've done to make the egg whites airy. Remember, the less you disturb beaten egg whites, the happier they are.

Storage of the Separated Egg

If you have leftover whites and yolks from the separated egg, they can be stored for later use. Store egg whites in a tightly covered container in the refrigerator for no longer than a week to 10 days. Unbroken yolks can be stored by covering them with a little water and keeping them in a covered dish. Drain the yolks and be sure to use within two to three days.

Egg whites can be frozen in closed containers. When you thaw them, measure out 2 to 3 tablespoons of egg white for each large grade A egg white needed. It is also handy to freeze egg whites in an ice cube tray, one white to each cube. Pop out the cubes and store them in a plastic bag in the freezer, for use one at a time.

Egg yolks must be stabilized with salt or sugar before freezing. Beat the yolks lightly before freezing, and then measure: For each measured cup of yolks, add one tablespoon of sugar for sweet dishes or one teaspoon of salt for savory dishes. Freeze the mixtures in airtight containers. Unless your memory is better than mine, it is a good idea to label the number of yolks in each container, and whether they are to be used in sweet or savory dishes.

Mousseline Omelettes

Of all omelettes, the mousseline is the least known. A favorite of mine, its creamy lightness is truly worth the extra effort of beating the eggs separately.

Of all the airy omelettes, the mousseline is most similar to the plain omelette. Like the plain omelette, a mousseline is cooked in an omelette pan. Sweet or savory, a mousseline omelette also may be filled and folded, though it is often served flat.

Unlike the French omelette, the mousseline is made from the separated egg. First, the egg yolks are beaten with seasonings and a little cream. Sometimes an extra egg yolk is added for extra richness. Then fluffy egg whites are incorporated into the yolk mixture. The combined mixture is poured into an ovenproof omelette pan and, to prevent sticking, a generous portion of butter is used. The mousseline omelette is pan-fried on the bottom, then broiled on top. The result is a high, round omelette which may be filled and folded, or served flat.

To dress up an unfilled mousseline omelette, make peaks with the mixture when you put it in the omelette pan. Sugar or cheese sprinkled on top before broiling makes a flavorful crust for the mousseline omelette.

Any of the fillings for the plain savory omelette can be used for the savory, cheese or herb mousseline omelettes. To fill the sweet mousseline omelette use any of the suggested fillings for the plain sweet omelette. The sweet mousseline omelette is elegant when spread with a simple jelly or jam. For fancier fixin's, try a sweet mousseline omelette folded over crème pâtissière (page 26) and fresh peaches. The bounty of nature is transformed into a sublime dessert.

Frequently a mousseline omelette which has been folded will crack because it is so thick. But the lack of perfect beauty in a cracked omelette is compensated for by its light flavor and texture. If your filled omelette is sweet, dust it with powdered sugar after it is folded. This dusting of sweetness covers a multitude of sins. If your filling is savory, garnish the omelette with a generous sprinkling of chopped fresh herbs.

The Mousseline Omelette

3 egg yolks
1 tablespoon cream
¼ teaspoon salt
⅛ teaspoon pepper, optional
2 egg whites
⅛ teaspoon salt
⅛ teaspoon cream of tartar (if not using a copper bowl)
1½ tablespoons unsalted butter

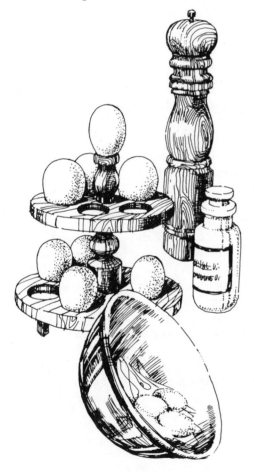

Turn on the broiler.

Beat the yolks with an electric mixer or a whisk until they are thick and mousse-like. Gradually add cream, salt and pepper until just incorporated.

Beat the egg whites with ⅛ teaspoon salt and the optional cream of tartar until the whites form stiff, moist peaks. Fold 1 cup of whites into the yolks to lighten them. Then, using a large whisk, fold the yolks into the remaining whites until the mixture is incorporated and pale yellow in color.

Put the butter into an 8-inch omelette pan and place the pan over medium temperature, swirling butter to melt. When melted, add egg mixture. Pull the mixture in from the sides with a metal spatula or spoon. Lift and fold the mixture into the center of the pan for about 30 seconds or until the mixture begins to thicken but is not yet set or cooked.

Use the spatula to spread the mixture until it is smooth on top. Place the pan under the broiler for about 30 to 45 seconds, until the omelette is lightly browned. Slip a spatula around the edge of the omelette and underneath it to be sure that it has loosened from the pan. Slide the cooked omelette out onto a plate so that the broiled top is showing. Serve flat.

If the omelette is to be filled, place the filling on half of the omelette and fold the other half over it. Garnish, if you wish, and serve.

NOTE: This recipe makes an omelette that is a very generous portion for one person and often feeds two or more. You can double it and make two omelettes, but do *not* try to make more than two. The airy mixture will deflate in the time it takes to make more than two omelettes. If you use a 10- to 12-inch omelette pan, double the recipe to make one large omelette. Quadruple the recipe to make two large omelettes.

Variations on the Mousseline Omelette

When you add the cream and seasonings to the yolks, add the listed ingredients in the following savory variations.

CHEESE MOUSSELINE OMELETTE

¼ cup grated cheese

Just before you put the omelette under the broiler, sprinkle it with 1 more tablespoon of grated cheese.

HERB MOUSSELINE OMELETTE

2 tablespoons chopped fresh herbs

SWEET MOUSSELINE OMELETTE

Substitute the listed ingredients for the ¼ teaspoon salt and ⅛ teaspoon pepper to create these sweet variations on the plain mousseline omelette.

1 to 2 tablespoons sugar
1 teaspoon vanilla or 1 tablespoon of any spirits (kirsch, Cointreau, brandy, framboise, rum, sherry etc.)

Just before you put the omelette under the broiler, sprinkle it with 1 teaspoon sugar.

CHOCOLATE MOUSSELINE OMELETTE

1 ounce unsweetened chocolate
2 tablespoons water
¼ cup sugar

Melt the chocolate in 2 tablespoons of water over very low heat. Do not boil. Then stir in the sugar. Add to the yolks. The omelette may take a minute or two of extra cooking.

The Omelette Soufflé

Somewhere between the omelette and the soufflé—closer to the soufflé—lies the omelette soufflé, a puffy, sweet dessert. Once cooked in a frying pan like a mousseline omelette, today an omelette soufflé is more likely to be baked in an oven like a soufflé.

The omelette soufflé is not quite a soufflé. It is lighter because it does not have the soufflé's heavier flour base. But it is cooked in an oval baking dish, which makes it look more like an omelette.

The omelette soufflé is similar to the mousseline omelette as well as the omelette and soufflé. In both dishes the egg whites are beaten separately and added just before cooking. The main difference between these two dishes is that the omelette soufflé is lighter and not as rich as a mousseline omelette. The lightness is a result of extra egg whites in the omelette soufflé. The mousseline omelette is richer because it has cream and often an extra egg yolk as well. The omelette soufflé is usually baked in the oven, while the mousseline omelette is prepared on top of the stove and then browned under the broiler.

Traditionally, the omelette soufflé is baked in a mound in an oval dish. Some of the mixture can be reserved and placed in a pastry bag to make decorative shapes on top of the soufflé. Or, you can make an indentation in the soufflé by pulling a knife down the middle of the uncooked mixture. Run the knife's point about 1 inch deep in the mixture. This indentation not only decorates the omelette soufflé, but helps to cook the inside of the omelette.

An omelette soufflé is faster to make than a soufflé. It cooks faster because it is not as deep a mixture. However, the omelette soufflé deflates more quickly because it lacks the flour base of a soufflé. To be at its best it should be prepared at eating time. Once it deflates, it cannot be revived. But on that rare occasion when you have a little left, it is still quite tasty reheated.

Omelette Soufflé

1 tablespoon butter
9 egg yolks
¾ cup sugar
¼ cup spirits (Grand Marnier,
   Amaretto, rum, kirsch, Kahlua,
   Cognac, framboise, etc.)
1 teaspoon vanilla extract
12 egg whites
⅛ teaspoon salt
¼ teaspoon cream of tartar (if not
   using a copper bowl)
2 teaspoons powdered sugar for
   decoration, if desired

Preheat oven to 375 degrees.

Grease a 2-by-10-by-17-inch oval au gratin pan or any attractive 2- to 2½-quart shallow baking dish with 1 tablespoon of butter. Beat the egg yolks for about a minute with an electric mixer or a whisk. Gradually add the sugar. When the mixture is thick and mousse-like, add the spirits and the vanilla. Beat about 30 seconds to incorporate.

Beat the egg whites with ⅛ teaspoon salt and the optional cream of tartar. Beat until they form stiff, moist peaks. Fold 1 cup of the whites into the yolk mixture to lighten it. Then, using a large whisk, fold the yolks into the remaining whites until the mixture is incorporated and a pale yellow.

In the buttered au gratin pan, heap the mixture in an oval-shaped mound about 4 inches high. Smooth the mixture with a spoon. Then, make an indentation lengthwise through the middle of the soufflé by running a knife's point about 1 inch deep into the uncooked mixture. Bake for 20 minutes until the soufflé is well puffed and browned. Use a sieve to dust with powdered sugar, if you wish. Serve the soufflé immediately.

Variations on the Omelette Soufflé

You can create myriad variations of this soufflé simply by varying the liqueurs. Gilding the lily with a dusting of confectioners' sugar and a fruit sauce (page 67) is an admirable idea.

CHOCOLATE OMELETTE SOUFFLÉ

2 ounces unsweetened chocolate
¼ cup water

Very slowly melt the chocolate in the water, using a small saucepan. Increase the sugar to 1 cup and add to the yolks. When the chocolate has melted, stir the chocolate mixture into the thick and mousse-like egg yolk and sugar mixture.

ALMOND OMELETTE SOUFFLÉ

2 tablespoons Amaretto or
   1 teaspoon almond extract
½ cup chopped almonds
1 teaspoon powdered sugar
1 tablespoon toasted almonds

Use Amaretto or almond extract for the spirits and fold the chopped almonds into the egg mixture before cooking. Dust with powdered sugar and sprinkle toasted almonds on top.

The Salzburger Nockerl

The Salzburger nockerl is a traditional sweet Austrian dessert which is similar to an omelette soufflé in its shape, size and baking method. This very light dish, made with twice as many whites as yolks, is most often baked in fluffy mounds in an oval container.

Because it has a bit of flour added to stabilize the mixture, the Salzburger nockerl is a tasty transition from the omelette soufflé to the soufflé. The flour stabilizes the airy mixture and allows it to "hold" longer, rather than collapse as the omelette soufflé will. If any Salzburger nockerl is left over (heaven forbid!), it can be reheated and eaten by the cook. It is not as puffy as when hot out of the oven, but it is still very good.

Lemon zest is the traditional flavoring of a Salzburger nockerl. The zest is the colored part of the citrus rind. This colored part gives flavor and, unlike the white part of the rind, leaves no bitter aftertaste. In a squeeze, you can substitute ½ teaspoon lemon extract.

Salzburger Nockerl

Serves 4 to 6 for dessert

1 tablespoon butter
3 egg yolks
¼ cup sugar
1 tablespoon flour
Zest of 1 lemon
6 egg whites
⅛ teaspoon salt
⅛ teaspoon cream of tartar (if not using a copper bowl)
1 teaspoon powdered sugar for decoration

Preheat oven to 425 degrees.

Generously butter a 2-by-8-by-10-inch oval au gratin pan or a 1½- to 2-quart shallow baking dish with 1 tablespoon butter. Sprinkle it with 1 tablespoon sugar.

Beat the egg yolks for about 1 minute with an electric mixer or whisk. Add the sugar, flour and lemon zest and beat until the mixture is thick and mousse-like.

Beat the egg whites with ⅛ teaspoon salt and the optional cream of tartar until they form stiff, moist peaks. Stir 1 cup of the whites into the yolk mixture to lighten the yolks. Then, using a large whisk, fold the yolks into the remaining whites until the mixture is incorporated and a pale yellow.

With a large spoon, heap the mixture into 3 large mounds in a baking dish. Bake for about 10 minutes or until lightly browned. Use a sieve to dust the nockerl with powdered sugar and serve immediately.

Soufflés

Secrets of the Soufflé

The soufflé is often called the prima donna of the culinary world, and like many of the chefs who create it, the soufflé has a reputation for being difficult. To master this creation, do not treat it like the mound of hot air that it really is. Instead try to understand a few of its secrets. Then the soufflé will make you as much of a star at the table as it is.

Composition of the Soufflé

A soufflé is not a complicated culinary creation at all. It is merely a thick sauce—enriched with egg yolks and heartily flavored—that puffs up to twice its size when it takes a big breath of airy egg whites and slips into a warm spot. So if you can make something as basic as a simple white sauce for macaroni and cheese, you have mastered the beginnings of a soufflé.

There are three parts to a soufflé: The base, the flavoring and the egg whites.

The base is usually a sauce. There are three types of sauce bases. An enriched sauce is commonly used for savory soufflés and some sweet soufflés. A *bouillie*, made with milk and flour or cornstarch, is most often used for sweet soufflés. A *crème pâtissière* (see page 26) is also used as a base for a sweet soufflé. Some fruit soufflés are not based on a sauce but on pureed fruit, to which a sugar syrup and beaten egg whites are added. I prefer to use the white sauce for savory soufflés and sweet liqueur soufflés. I use a cornstarch *bouillie* for fruit and chocolate soufflés.

The flavoring gives the soufflé its identity. Without the addition of a vegetable, fruit, meat, liqueur or some other flavor, the soufflé would be a beauty with no personality. So that the egg whites can lift the flavor to the sky, foods used in a soufflé should be either finely chopped or puréed. I prefer the texture of finely chopped food. Since the soufflé will form a cloud around the flavoring and only allow it to heat, the flavoring should be cooked, if necessary, before it is added to the base. Food such as tomatoes, avocado and cheese do not need cooking. Be heavy-handed with seasonings because when the soufflé is cooked, the mixture will expand to a greater volume and the intensity of its flavor will diminish.

The egg whites and air give the soufflé base the power to rise to great heights. The word soufflé comes from the French verb *souffler*, "to breathe," and when the egg whites are properly whisked they do take a big breath of air. Chemically, the dramatic enlargement is caused by the expansion of the air bubbles in the egg whites when they are heated.

A Skilled Hand

The magnificence of a soufflé is mainly the result of how well the egg whites have been beaten and how carefully they have been folded into the base. (See *The Separated Egg*, pages 38-40, for complete explanations of both techniques.)

Equipment

The only pieces of equipment you need for a soufflé are: A saucepan and whisk for making the base; a copper bowl and balloon whisk, or a good quality electric mixer, for beating the whites; and a straight-sided bowl with a high collar for cooking the soufflé.

Use a heavy-bottomed saucepan for making the white sauce so that the roux (butter and flour) will not burn before it cooks. A whisk is best for stirring because it incorporates the roux faster and keeps it from lumping. In making the base, stir the mixture with a smaller, less flexible whisk than the one used for beating egg whites.

For beating egg whites use a copper bowl and a balloon whisk, or a good quality electric mixer.

Use a straight-sided soufflé dish to give more stability to the soufflé as it rises. Soufflé dishes are available in many materials: ovenproof china and glass, pottery and copper. I prefer ovenproof china or glass, though pottery and copper can be interesting and beautiful. Glass is certainly impressive because it makes the soufflé look like a free-standing mound. Because a pottery soufflé dish may retain heat longer, it sometimes makes cooking unpredictable, so get to know your soufflé dish and its cooking characteristics.

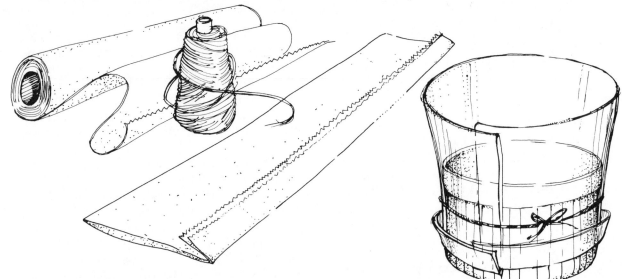

Preparing the Dish

Butter the dish with about 1 tablespoon of butter. If you are making a soufflé with cheese, sprinkle 1 tablespoon grated cheese into the dish. Shake the dish so that the cheese coats the bottom and sides. This makes a flavorful crust on the outside of the soufflé. If you are making a sweet soufflé, sprinkle the buttered dish with 1 tablespoon sugar. Then turn the dish upside down and tap it to remove any excess.

A collar for the soufflé bowl extends the capacity of the dish, gives the soufflé stability as it rises, and keeps it from spilling over into the oven. To make a collar, cut a piece of wax paper or aluminum foil long enough to go around the soufflé dish with a slight overlap. Fold the paper in half lengthwise. Butter one side of the wax paper with 1 tablespoon of butter and wrap the buttered side of the paper securely around the soufflé dish, buttered side in and folded side down. Overlap the collar slightly. Tie the wax paper collar securely around the dish with a piece of string so that several inches of the collar stand above the dish.

Measurements

In my cooking classes and also in this book, I emphasize improvisation, creative selection of ingredients and getting a feeling for the right texture and result. In soufflé-making, creativity in choice of ingredients is commendable, but it is important to stick to the proportions in the basic soufflé recipes. Much of the success of the soufflé depends on the relationship of the quantities. Be careful, because too great a quantity of flavoring will make the soufflé too heavy to rise.

Making It Ahead

One reason why so many cooks stand in awe of the soufflé is its last-minute preparation. However, the soufflé can be partially prepared or even totally prepared ahead of time. I prefer partial advance preparation.

Prepare the soufflé dish. Make the base and add the flavorings. Set aside. Then, 10 minutes before it is time to cook the soufflé (about 45 minutes before serving time), reheat the base to warm it. Do not overheat. Meanwhile, turn up the music so that your guests will not hear the clatter of your whisk and copper bowl, and whisk the whites. I promise that this will keep you from your guests only for about 10 minutes.

A soufflé can also be made ahead and completely assembled. In *From Julia Child's Kitchen*, Julia Child suggests putting a soufflé in a warm, draft-free spot and holding it for up to two hours. I have held one in a warm spot uncovered for this long. Though it is sometimes risky to hold a soufflé, I have had good results with this method.

The Upper Crust

The outside of a baked soufflé will have a crust after it is baked. However, for a browner, crustier upper crust on a savory soufflé, sprinkle the top with one tablespoon of grated cheese just before it goes into the oven. Sprinkle one teaspoon of sugar on a sweet soufflé.

A Soufflé's Place in the Oven

Always place a soufflé on the bottom rack of a preheated oven. In this place, your rising star will not hit the ceiling of your oven. (It has happened before!) In addition, when a soufflé is placed near the bottom heating element, it gets the initial kick it needs to start its climb.

To Test for Doneness

Do not disturb the soufflé by opening and closing the door to check on its progress until the last few minutes of cooking. There are several ways to know if a soufflé is ready.

When it is nearly ready you will begin to notice its aroma. Then test it by kicking the oven! Unless the oven is standing very firmly on the floor, it will move slightly and you can tell how the soufflé is getting along. If the soufflé shakes in a solid manner it is ready. Like a belly dancer, a soufflé should shimmy in one smooth motion, not jiggle in all directions. More timid souls can reach into the oven with a pot holder and gently pat the bowl. A soufflé that is properly done will be firm and golden brown.

Some people like a soft, sauce-like center to spoon over each serving. If this is your preference, remove the soufflé from the oven about five minutes early. When you remove it early, the center will sink slightly and the soufflé will deflate more quickly—so serve it with haste.

The Presentation

The audience must always wait for a soufflé to make its grand entrance. Remember, it will not wait for them. So have your guests seated and ready before you bring the soufflé out of the oven. If your timing is a little off, turn the oven off when the soufflé is done. The soufflé will hold for about five minutes in the oven and still be hot under the collar.

Remove the collar before rushing the soufflé to the table. Serve it proudly and be sure that each portion includes both the golden brown crust and the creamy center.

Accompaniments

A well-cooked soufflé is so moist and creamy that a sauce is unnecessary. However, a Mornay sauce, tomato sauce or even Madeira sauce is a good accompaniment to many savory soufflés. Sweet soufflés are especially delicious with compatible fruit sauces (page 67).

A soufflé can be a first course, main course, dessert or a full meal. For a light supper or lunch, serve a savory soufflé with a clear soup, a salad or steamed fresh vegetables, cool, dry white wine and a fruit dessert.

The Basic Savory Soufflé

The following is the basic soufflé recipe based on a white sauce made from a roux (butter and flour cooked together) and a liquid (usually milk). All of the savory soufflés in this book are based on this formula.

BASE:
3 tablespoons butter
3 tablespoons flour
1 cup liquid (examples: milk, chicken or beef broth, clam juice, beer, wine)
4 egg yolks

FLAVORING:
Up to 1 cup meat, cheese, vegetable, seafood, finely chopped (1¼ cup may be used if a portion of the flavoring is cheese)

AIR:
6 egg whites
¼ teaspoon cream of tartar (if not using a copper bowl)
⅛ teaspoon salt

Preheat the oven to 375 degrees and remove all the racks but the bottom one.

Prepare a 1½ quart soufflé dish.

Heat the butter in a saucepan at medium temperature. Do not allow the butter to brown. Remove the pan from the burner, add the flour to make a roux and whisk to incorporate thoroughly. Return to the burner and cook at medium temperature for about 1 minute. Do *not* brown the roux. Remove from the heat, add the liquid gradually and blend with a whisk. Return to medium-high heat and bring to a boil, whisking constantly. Continue whisking and boiling for 1 minute to make a thick sauce.

Remove from the heat and whisk the mixture to cool it for about a minute, so that the egg yolks will not poach when added. Whisk in the egg yolks, one at a time. Add the flavoring and combine.

Beat the egg whites in a clean dry bowl with a pinch of salt and ¼ teaspoon of the optional cream of tartar. When the whites stand in stiff, moist peaks, fold about 1 cup of the whites into the warm base to lighten it. Then add the base down the inside of the bowl of egg whites. Fold together lightly until the mixture is just incorporated.

Scoop the soufflé mixture into a prepared soufflé dish. Smooth the surface of the soufflé with a spoon. (The dish should be almost full.) Place the soufflé in a 375-degree preheated oven, on the bottom rack. Cook for 30 to 35 minutes until the soufflé has risen 2 to 3 inches above the bowl and is firm and brown on top.

Remove from the oven, remove the collar, and rush it to the table.

SOUFFLÉS FOR THE MASSES

A 1½-quart soufflé serves 4 people generously, or 6 people lightly. A 2-quart soufflé dish serves 6 to 8 people. To fill a 2-quart soufflé dish, increase the proportions for a 1½-quart soufflé by one third.

4 tablespoons butter	1¼ cups flavoring
4 tablespoons flour	8 egg whites
1¼ cup liquid	½ teaspoon cream of tartar
5 egg yolks	⅛ teaspoon salt

If you want to make soufflé for the masses, make more soufflés, not *bigger* soufflés. Soufflés made in quantities greater than 2 quarts are too heavy to rise properly or cook evenly.

If you want individual soufflés, divide the mixture into smaller soufflé bowls (1 to 1½ cups) and cook for about 20 to 25 minutes. For a soufflé for 2, use a 1-quart bowl and reduce the 1½-quart soufflé proportions by one third.

2 tablespoons butter	⅔ cup flavoring
2 tablespoons flour	5 egg whites
⅔ cup liquid	¼ teaspoon cream of tartar
3 egg yolks	⅛ teaspoon salt

Flavoring the Soufflé

The basic savory soufflé can be varied in a number of ways. All of the flavorings suggested in this section are simply variations of the basic savory recipe.

Most of the flavorings are added to the sauce after the egg yolks, as directed in the basic recipe. However, a few additions are better made at other points. These changes will be noted in shortened forms of the basic recipe.

Cheese is one of the most popular and classic flavorings for a soufflé. It is an ingredient used in many different soufflés—not just in cheese soufflés. Cheese is one of the ingredients that does not go into the sauce. When you add cheese to a soufflé, sprinkle it onto the beaten egg whites. If you add cheese to the base, it will become so heavy that incorporating the mixtures will be difficult and the resulting soufflé will not be as light.

When a soufflé calls for ingredients that need to be sautéed lightly—such as onions, mushrooms or garlic—you can cook them in the butter used for the roux, before the flour is added. Then proceed to make the sauce. This eliminates an extra pan for the cook to wash.

Cheese Soufflé

The first cheese soufflé that I ever made was under the tutelage of Irena Chalmers. Here is my version of her cheese soufflé.

3 tablespoons butter
3 tablespoons flour
1 cup milk
4 egg yolks
6 egg whites
⅛ teaspoon salt
¼ teaspoon cream of tartar (if not using a copper bowl)

FLAVORING:
2 teaspoons Dijon mustard
½ teaspoon salt
½ teaspoon freshly ground pepper
¼ teaspoon nutmeg
⅛ teaspoon cayenne pepper
½ cup grated Parmesan cheese
½ cup grated Gruyère cheese

Preheat the oven to 375 degrees.

Prepare a 1½-quart soufflé dish.

Heat the butter. Whisk in the flour. Gradually whisk in the milk and cook until the mixture thickens. Remove from heat, and whisk in yolks one at a time. Stir in all the flavorings except the cheeses.

Beat the egg whites with ⅛ teaspoon salt and the optional cream of tartar until stiff, moist peaks form. Lighten the base mixture with 1 cup of the beaten egg whites. Fold the base mixture and cheese (reserving 1 tablespoon Parmesan) into the egg whites. Scoop the mixture into the soufflé dish. Sprinkle the unbaked soufflé with 1 tablespoon of grated Parmesan cheese. Bake for 30 to 35 minutes.

NOTE: For a change of flavor, substitute other cheeses for the Gruyère and Parmesan. Try Appenzell or cheddar.

Variations on the Cheese Soufflé

CHEESE AND ONION SOUFFLÉ

½ cup finely chopped onion

Add the onion to the melted butter. Cook until the onions are soft but not brown. Then whisk in the flour.

CHEESE AND HERB SOUFFLÉ

1 to 2 tablespoons fresh, chopped herbs or 1 to 2 teaspoons dried herbs (suggestions: winter savory, dill weed, chives, parsley, thyme, chervil, marjoram, rosemary, sage)

Add the herbs to the base when you add the seasonings.

NOTE: You may use just one herb, or a compatible combination of any of the herbs that totals 2 tablespoons. If you choose a strong herb, such as rosemary or sage, use a lesser quantity.

Garden Vegetable Soufflé (Corn Soufflé)

A garden vegetable soufflé is a wonderful way to capture summer's bounty. Pluck fresh vegetables from your garden or the greengrocer's shelf, and mince them well for the airy soufflé mixture.

Try different combinations, and be sure to add an onion—the most sociable vegetable of all. The onion blends well with every other vegetable and makes all other vegetables taste even better. This particular garden vegetable soufflé is based on corn.

3 tablespoons butter
3 tablespoons flour
1 cup milk, or ½ cup milk and
** ½ cup chicken broth**
4 egg yolks
6 egg whites
⅛ teaspoon salt
¼ teaspoon cream of tartar (if not
** using a copper bowl)**

FLAVORING:
¼ cup minced onion
1 cup fresh uncooked corn, cut from
** the cob**
1 teaspoon salt
½ teaspoon nutmeg

Preheat the oven to 375 degrees.

Prepare a 1½-quart soufflé dish.

Heat the butter. Add the minced onion and cook until it is soft but not brown. Whisk in the flour. Gradually whisk in the liquid and cook until the mixture thickens. Remove from heat. Then whisk in the yolks one at a time. Stir in the corn and seasonings.

Beat the egg whites with ⅛ teaspoon of salt and the optional cream of tartar until stiff, moist peaks form. Lighten the corn mixture with 1 cup of the beaten egg whites. Fold the corn mixture into the egg whites. Scoop the mixture into the soufflé dish. Bake for 30 to 35 minutes.

NOTE: Add less salt when using chicken broth.

Variations on the Garden Vegetable Soufflé

In the following variations on the Corn Soufflé, substitute the suggested vegetables for the corn and add the cheeses at the point when you add the beaten egg whites.

SPINACH SOUFFLÉ

1 cup chopped cooked spinach
¼ cup grated Parmesan or cheddar
   cheese

CAULIFLOWER SOUFFLÉ

1 cup cooked, finely chopped
   cauliflower
¼ cup grated Parmesan or Gruyère
   cheese

BROCCOLI SOUFFLÉ

1 cup cooked, finely chopped
   broccoli
1 tablespoon fresh dill weed or
   2 teaspoons dried
¼ cup grated Parmesan, Gruyère or
   Appenzell cheese

ZUCCHINI SOUFFLÉ

1 cup grated raw zucchini
2 tablespoons fresh dill weed or
   2 teaspoons dried

ASPARAGUS SOUFFLÉ

1 cup cooked, finely chopped
   asparagus
1 tablespoon orange zest (optional)
2 tablespoons chopped walnuts
   (optional)

AVOCADO, ARTICHOKE AND TOMATO SOUFFLÉ

⅓ cup finely chopped marinated
   artichoke hearts
⅓ cup peeled, seeded and finely
   chopped tomato, well drained
⅓ cup finely chopped avocado
¼ cup grated Gruyère cheese

Follow the Corn Soufflé directions, but omit the nutmeg entirely and reduce the salt to ½ teaspoon. Add the cheese at the point when you add the beaten egg whites.

CARROT SOUFFLÉ

1 cup cooked, finely minced carrots
2 tablespoons chopped fresh chervil
   or 2 teaspoons dried

MIXED VEGETABLE SOUFFLÉ

1 cup total of a cooked, chopped,
   tasty medley of vegetables such as
   carrots, peas and zucchini
¼ cup Gruyère or Parmesan cheese
   (optional)

Wild Rice and Rosemary Soufflé

Wild rice is one of America's greatest gifts to the world of food. It is not really a rice but a grass grown in Minnesota.

3 tablespoons butter
3 tablespoons flour
1 cup milk, or chicken or beef broth
4 egg yolks
6 egg whites
⅛ teaspoon salt
¼ teaspoon cream of tartar (if not using a copper bowl)

FLAVORING:
½ cup minced onion
1 cup cooked wild rice
2 tablespoons vermouth
2 teaspoons chopped, fresh rosemary, or 1 teaspoon dried
1 teaspoon salt
½ teaspoon freshly ground pepper

Preheat oven to 375 degrees.

Prepare a 1½-quart soufflé dish.

Heat the butter. Add the minced onion and cook until soft but not brown. Whisk in the flour. Gradually whisk in the liquid and cook until the mixture thickens. Remove from heat, and whisk in yolks one at a time. Stir in rice, vermouth and seasonings.*

Beat the egg whites with ⅛ teaspoon salt and the optional cream of tartar until stiff, moist peaks form. Lighten the rice mixture with 1 cup of the beaten egg whites. Fold the rice mixture into the egg whites. Scoop the mixture into the soufflé dish. Bake for 30 to 35 minutes.

Clam Oreganata Soufflé

3 tablespoons butter
3 tablespoons flour
½ cup milk + ½ cup clam juice
(reserved from drained clams)
4 egg yolks
6 egg whites
⅛ teaspoon salt
¼ teaspoon cream of tartar (if not using a copper bowl)

FLAVORING:
¾ cup tomatoes peeled, seeded, and chopped into small pieces
6½-ounce can minced clams, drained (reserve liquid)
2 tablespoons chopped onion
1 tablespoon fresh chopped parsley
1 tablespoon fresh chopped oregano
½ teaspoon salt
½ teaspoon pepper
¼ cup grated Parmesan cheese
¼ cup grated Gruyère cheese
1 tablespoon grated Parmesan cheese

Preheat oven to 375 degrees.

Prepare a 1½-quart soufflé dish.

Heat the butter. Add the onions and cook until soft but not brown. Whisk in the flour. Gradually whisk in the milk and clam juice and cook until the mixture thickens. Remove from heat, and add yolks one at a time. Stir in the tomatoes, clams and seasonings.

Beat the egg whites with ⅛ teaspoon salt and the optional cream of tartar until stiff, moist peaks form. Lighten the clam mixture with 1 cup of the beaten egg whites. Fold the clam mixture and grated cheese into the egg whites. Reserve 1 tablespoon of the cheese. Scoop the mixture into the soufflé dish. Sprinkle the unbaked soufflé with the reserved grated Parmesan cheese. Bake for 30 to 35 minutes.

Scallop and Chervil Soufflé

Serves 4 to 6

Bay scallops are usually the size of the end of your little finger. They are so small that they do not have to be cut for this recipe.

3 tablespoons butter
3 tablespoons flour
½ cup milk + ½ cup scallop juice
  (or enough to make 1 cup)
4 egg yolks
6 egg whites
⅛ teaspoon salt
¼ teaspoon cream of tartar (if not
  using a copper bowl)

FLAVORING:
2 scallions, whites and tops finely
  chopped (about ¼ cup)
1 cup raw bay scallops or chopped
  sea scallops (about ½ pound)
2 tablespoons vermouth
1 tablespoon lemon juice
1 tablespoon chopped fresh chervil
  or parsley or chives
1 teaspoon salt
⅛ teaspoon pepper

Preheat oven to 375 degrees.

Prepare a 1½-quart soufflé dish.

Heat the butter. Add the scallions and cook until soft but not brown. Whisk in the flour. Gradually whisk in the liquid and cook until the mixture thickens. Remove from heat, and add the yolks one at a time. Stir in the raw scallops, vermouth, lemon juice, chervil, salt and pepper.

Beat the egg whites with ⅛ teaspoon salt and the optional cream of tartar until stiff, moist peaks form. Lighten the scallop mixture with 1 cup of the beaten egg whites. Fold the scallop mixture into the egg whites. Scoop the mixture into the soufflé dish. Bake for 30 to 35 minutes.

Curried Shrimp and Asparagus Soufflé

Serves 4 to 6

3 tablespoons butter
3 tablespoons flour
1 cup milk
4 egg yolks
6 egg whites
⅛ teaspoon salt
¼ teaspoon cream of tartar (if not
    using a copper bowl)

FLAVORING:
¼ cup minced onion
½ cup chopped cooked shrimp
½ cup chopped cooked asparagus
2 tablespoons dry sherry
2 teaspoons curry powder
1 teaspoon salt
½ teaspoon freshly ground pepper

Preheat oven to 375 degrees.

Prepare a 1½-quart soufflé dish.

Heat the butter. Add the onion and cook until soft but not brown. Whisk in the flour. Gradually whisk in the milk and cook until the mixture thickens. Remove from the heat, and add the yolks one at a time. Stir in the shrimp, asparagus, sherry and seasonings.

Beat the egg whites with ⅛ teaspoon salt and the optional cream of tartar until stiff, moist peaks form. Lighten the shrimp mixture with 1 cup of the beaten egg whites. Fold the shrimp mixture into the egg whites. Scoop the mixture into the soufflé dish. Bake for 30 to 35 minutes.

NOTE: A half cup chopped, cooked crab or lobster may be substituted for the shrimp.

Smithfield Ham and Zucchini Soufflé

Serves 4 to 6

3 tablespoons butter
3 tablespoons flour
1 cup milk
4 egg yolks
6 egg whites
⅛ teaspoon salt
¼ teaspoon cream of tartar (if not
    using a copper bowl)

FLAVORING:
¾ cup shredded, uncooked zucchini
¼ cup finely chopped Smithfield
    ham, country ham or prosciutto
½ teaspoon salt
½ teaspoon pepper
¼ cup Parmesan cheese, grated

Preheat the oven to 375 degrees.

Prepare a 1½-quart soufflé dish.

Heat the butter. Whisk in the flour. Gradually whisk in the milk and cook until the mixture thickens. Remove from the heat, and add the yolks one at a time. Stir in zucchini, ham, salt and pepper.*

Beat the egg whites with ⅛ teaspoon salt and the optional cream of tartar until stiff, moist peaks form. Lighten the zucchini and ham mixture with 1 cup of the beaten egg whites. Fold the base mixture and ¼ cup Parmesan cheese (reserving 1 tablespoon) into the egg whites. Scoop the mixture into the soufflé dish. Sprinkle the unbaked soufflé with the reserved 1 tablespoon grated Parmesan cheese. Bake for 30 to 35 minutes.

NOTE: Three-fourths cup chopped, cooked spinach or finely chopped, cooked broccoli may be substituted for the zucchini.

Chicken, Mushroom and Tarragon Soufflé

Serves 4 to 6

3 tablespoons butter
3 tablespoons flour
1 cup milk
4 egg yolks
6 egg whites
⅛ teaspoon salt
¼ teaspoon cream of tartar (if not using a copper bowl)

FLAVORING:
1 clove garlic, minced
¼ cup minced onion
¼ cup chopped mushrooms
2 tablespoons vermouth
½ cup chopped cooked chicken
1 tablespoon chopped fresh tarragon, or 1 teaspoon dried
1 teaspoon salt
½ teaspoon freshly ground pepper

Preheat oven to 375 degrees.

Prepare a 1½-quart soufflé dish.

Heat the butter. Cook the garlic and onions in butter until the onions are soft but not brown. Add the mushrooms and cook for 1 minute. Whisk in the flour. Gradually whisk in the milk and cook until the mixture thickens. Remove from heat, and whisk in the yolks one at a time. Stir in the vermouth, chicken and seasonings.*

Beat the egg whites with ⅛ teaspoon salt and the optional cream of tartar until stiff, moist peaks form. Lighten the chicken mixture with 1 cup of the beaten egg whites. Fold the chicken mixture into the egg whites. Scoop the mixture into the soufflé dish. Bake for 30 to 35 minutes.

Variations on the Chicken, Mushroom and Tarragon Soufflé

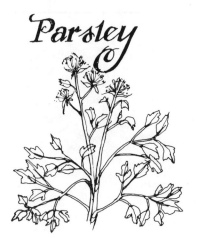

CHICKEN HERB SOUFFLÉ

Substitute an equal amount of either dill weed, oregano, thyme or rosemary for the tarragon in the preceding soufflé.

MUSHROOM TARRAGON SOUFFLÉ

Increase the mushrooms to ¾ cup and delete the chicken.

HAM, MUSHROOM AND DILL WEED SOUFFLÉ

Substitute ½ cup chopped cooked ham for the chicken and substitute 1 tablespoon of dill weed for the tarragon.

SMOKED TURKEY WITH CHIVES SOUFFLÉ

Substitute an equal amount of turkey for the chicken, and substitute an equal amount of chives for the tarragon.

Sweet Soufflés

Spirited Soufflés

Of all the sweet soufflés, those with a cream sauce base and a liqueur flavoring are the lightest and most aromatic. The same method is used for making liqueur soufflés and savory soufflés. See Basic Savory Soufflé (page 52) for more detailed instructions.

Fruit Soufflés

Fruit soufflés based on the basic cream sauce tend to be too moist and heavy and therefore do not rise properly. In *From Julia Child's Kitchen,* Julia Child suggests using a bouillie sauce as a base for some soufflés. I definitely have found that a bouillie sauce works better than a cream sauce for fruit soufflés. A bouillie sauce is made by combining a liquid and cornstarch and then boiling it until it thickens to a slightly thicker consistency than a cream sauce. Then the yolks are added. No butter is used, so the base is not as moist as a cream base.

   To make it easier for the soufflé to rise, use finely chopped or thinly sliced fruits. Pureed fruits are too heavy to use in the same proportions as those listed in the following fruit soufflé recipe. If the fruit is especially juicy, drain it. You may use the fruit juice as a liquid instead of the milk. Since egg whites will rise and the intensity of the flavors of the soufflés will be diluted, over-sweeten.

   Because fruit soufflés are heavier, they need a broader foundation. It is best to use a 1½-quart soufflé dish that has a wider diameter than standard; or, better yet, use a 2-quart soufflé dish.

Chocolate Soufflés

Chocolate soufflés, like fruit soufflés, are too thick and moist to use with a cream sauce base. The bouillie base used for fruit soufflés is better.

   For a flavorful crust on any of the sweet soufflés, sprinkle 1 tablespoon of sugar on top of the unbaked soufflé.

The Spirited Soufflé

3 tablespoons butter
3 tablespoons flour
1 cup milk
4 egg yolks
6 egg whites
⅛ teaspoon salt
¼ teaspoon cream of tartar (if not
   using a copper bowl)
1 tablespoon sugar

FLAVORING:
½ cup sugar
¼ cup liqueur
⅛ teaspoon nutmeg (optional)
⅛ teaspoon salt

Preheat oven to 375 degrees.

Prepare a 1½-quart soufflé dish.

Heat the butter. Whisk in the flour. Gradually whisk in the milk and cook until the mixture thickens. Remove from heat, and add yolks one at a time. Stir in sugar, liqueur, nutmeg and ⅛ teaspoon salt.

Beat the egg whites with ⅛ teaspoon salt and the optional cream of tartar until soft peaks form. Add 1 tablespoon sugar and continue beating until the egg whites form stiff, moist peaks. Lighten the liqueur mixture with 1 cup of the beaten egg whites. Fold the liqueur mixture into the egg whites. Scoop the mixture into the soufflé dish. Bake for 30 to 35 minutes.

NOTE: The spirits you use can be rum; orange liqueur; apricot, apple, pear or peach brandy; sherry—or whatever you fancy.

Serve with an appropriate fruit sauce.

Fruit Sauce

Spirited soufflés are delicious with fruit sauces.

1 cup pureed fruit, sieved if
   necessary to remove seeds
1 to 3 tablespoons sugar, to taste
2 tablespoons liqueur or rum
   (optional)

Heat the fruit. Add the sugar to taste and any spirits. Stir to dissolve the sugar.

NOTE: Sugar and spirits may be added to cold pureed fruit and served as a cold sauce on cold soufflés.

Basic Fruit Soufflé

BASE:
4 tablespoons cornstarch
1 cup milk
4 egg yolks
½ cup sugar

FLAVORING:
Up to 1½ cups chopped or thinly
    sliced fruit
1 teaspoon vanilla, and often other
    flavorings

AIR:
6 egg whites
⅛ teaspoon salt
¼ teaspoon cream of tartar (if not
    using a copper bowl)
1 tablespoon sugar

Preheat oven to 375 degrees.

Prepare a 2-quart soufflé dish.

Put 4 tablespoons of cornstarch into a medium-sized saucepan. Add ⅓ cup of the milk and combine until smooth. Gradually add the remaining milk, whisking until well blended. Cook the mixture over medium-high heat, stirring constantly until mixture thickens. Whisk rapidly until the mixture is smooth. The base will be very thick.

Remove from heat and allow to cool a minute so that the yolks will not poach when they are added. Whisk in the egg yolks one at a time. Gradually add ½ cup sugar and stir until well blended. Add the flavorings.

Beat the egg whites in a clean, dry bowl with ⅛ teaspoon salt and ¼ teaspoon optional cream of tartar until they form soft peaks. Gradually add 1 tablespoon of sugar and continue beating until the mixture forms stiff, moist peaks. Fold about 1 cup of the whites into the warm base to lighten the mixture. Then pour the mixture down the inside of the egg white bowl alongside the stiffly beaten whites. Then gently fold together with a large whisk so you do not deflate the whites.

Scoop the mixture into a prepared soufflé dish. Smooth the top surface of the soufflé with a spoon. The bowl should be almost full. Place it in the oven on the bottom rack and cook for 30 to 45 minutes until the soufflé has risen 2 to 3 inches above the bowl and is brown and firm.

Take it from the oven, remove the collar and serve immediately.

Variations on the Fruit Soufflé

Use the following suggested ingredients as the flavoring in the Basic Fruit Soufflé.

STRAWBERRY OR RASPBERRY SOUFFLÉ

1½ cups sliced strawberries or
    raspberries
2 tablespoons Grand Marnier or
    framboise
1 teaspoon vanilla

NOTE: If you are using frozen berries, use them unsweetened and drained.

MANGO SOUFFLÉ

1½ cups thin mango slices,
    quartered
1 teaspoon vanilla
2 tablespoons Grand Marnier

BANANA AND ORANGE SOUFFLÉ

½ cup milk and ½ cup orange juice
    instead of 1 cup milk

FLAVORING:
1½ cups thinly sliced and halved
    bananas sprinkled with
    1 tablespoon lemon juice
¼ cup finely chopped almonds
¼ cup rum
1 teaspoon vanilla

BLUEBERRY SOUFFLÉ

1½ cups whole blueberries
2 tablespoons rum or Amaretto
1 teaspoon vanilla

PEAR AND WALNUT SOUFFLÉ

1¼ cups thin pear slices, quartered
¼ cup finely chopped walnuts
2 tablespoons pear brandy
1 teaspoon vanilla

PEACH SOUFFLÉ

1½ cups thin peach slices, quartered
2 tablespoons peach brandy, rum or
   Grand Marnier
1 teaspoon vanilla

SWEET POTATO AND BOURBON SOUFFLÉ

The sweet potato is not a fruit, but if you treat it like one, it makes a delicious dessert. Pumpkin may be substituted for sweet potato in this recipe.

1½ cups coarsely grated sweet
   potato
2 tablespoons butter
¼ cup finely chopped almonds
¼ cup bourbon or rum
1 teaspoon cinnamon
1 teaspoon vanilla

Cook the sweet potatoes in 2 tablespoons of butter for about 5 minutes. Do not brown. Add to the soufflé with the other flavorings.

Chocolate Orange Soufflé

BASE:
4 tablespoons cornstarch
1 cup milk
4 egg yolks
½ cup sugar

FLAVORING:
4 ounces semi-sweet chocolate bits
Zest of 1 orange
2 tablespoons Grand Marnier
1 teaspoon vanilla

AIR:
7 egg whites
¼ teaspoon cream of tartar
⅛ teaspoon salt
1 tablespoon sugar

Preheat oven to 375 degrees.

Prepare a 2-quart soufflé dish.

Put 4 tablespoons of cornstarch into a medium-sized saucepan. Add ⅓ cup milk and combine until smooth. Add the remaining milk, whisking until well blended. Cook the mixture over medium-high heat, stirring until the mixture thickens. Whisk rapidly until smooth. The base will be very thick. Remove from heat and allow to cool a minute so the yolks will not poach when they are added. Whisk in the 4 egg yolks, one at a time. Gradually add the ½ cup of sugar and stir until well blended. Add the chocolate bits and stir until the chocolate melts. Add the other flavorings.

Beat the egg whites in a clean, dry bowl with ⅛ teaspoon salt and ¼ teaspoon optional cream of tartar until they form soft peaks. Gradually add 1 tablespoon of sugar and continue beating until the mixture forms stiff, moist peaks. Fold about 1 cup of the whites into the warm base to lighten the mixture. Then pour the mixture down the inside of the egg-white bowl alongside the stiffly beaten whites. Gently fold together with a large whisk so that you do not deflate the whites.

Scoop the mixture into a prepared soufflé dish. Smooth the top surface of the soufflé with a spoon. The bowl should be almost full. Place it in the oven on the bottom rack and cook for 30 to 45 minutes until the soufflé has risen 2 to 3 inches above the bowl and is brown and firm.

Take it from the oven, remove the collar and serve immediately.

NOTE: Omit the orange zest and Grand Marnier for a delicious plain chocolate soufflé.

Variations on the Chocolate Orange Soufflé

Substitute the following ingredients for the orange zest and Grand Marnier in the Chocolate Orange Soufflé.

CHOCOLATE RUM SOUFFLÉ

¼ cup rum

CHOCOLATE NUT SOUFFLÉ

¼ cup finely chopped nuts
   (hazelnuts, pecans, walnuts or
   almonds)
2 tablespoons rum or Amaretto

CHOCOLATE MOCHA SOUFFLÉ

¼ cup double-strength coffee
1 tablespoon Kahlua

Roulades

A roulade is a rolled soufflé, baked in a shallow, rectangular pan, spread with a filling and rolled up like a jelly roll. Savory or sweet, like its sister the soufflé, the roulade is a delicious light roll to serve as an hors d'oeuvre, main course or dessert. It is more convenient than the soufflé because it can be made ahead, refrigerated and reheated if necessary. It can even be frozen.

A roulade has two parts—the flat soufflé and the filling. The flat soufflé is a flavored wrapper that encloses a filling, just as the cake of a jelly roll wraps around the jam filling. This flat soufflé can have different flavorings—spinach, mushroom or even sugar—just as the cake of a jelly roll can be flavored with orange, lemon or chocolate. The filling of a roulade can be anything you choose—mushrooms in a cream sauce, beef tips or crabmeat, just as the filling of a jelly roll can be made from red-currant jelly, orange marmalade, pear preserves or other ingredients.

These two parts—the flat soufflé and the roulade filling—give the roulade its versatility; you can vary each part to create a different dish.

Preparing the Pan

The same utensils are used to make a roulade and a soufflé. Just use a jelly-roll pan instead of a soufflé bowl. A jelly-roll pan is a baking sheet with a one-inch lip on all sides.

To prepare the pan: Butter a 10-by-17-inch jelly-roll pan. Line it with a sheet of wax paper, leaving about two inches of paper hanging over each end of the pan. Butter the top of the paper liberally.

Removing the Roulade from the Pan

Once the roulade is baked, allow it to cool on a cake rack for five minutes. Then it is ready to turn out of the pan. (See diagram on page 75.)

Cut two sheets of wax paper that are six inches longer than the roulade. Place them on top of the roulade. Overlap the long sides of the wax paper for added strength. Position them so that about three inches of wax paper hang over the sides and ends of the pan. To remove the baked roulade: Grasp the wax paper and the ends of the jelly-roll pan firmly together with both hands and then quickly invert the roulade on top of a counter with the fresh wax paper underneath. Remove the pan and allow to cool for five minutes. Peel the baked wax paper off the roulade. Trim away any rough or brittle edges of the cooked roulade.

Filling and Rolling the Roulade

Spread the filling on the roulade carefully so as not to tear it. To make rolling easier, leave an un-filled portion of the roulade (about one-fourth of the whole roulade) down the long side. To roll, begin on the unfilled long side. With the aid of the wax paper, gently lift and roll the roulade jelly-roll fashion. Roll or slide it onto a serving board or platter.

The top of the roulade may crack while baking and sometimes it cracks while you are rolling it. If this happens, just pat it and push the cracks together. A sprinkling of chopped fresh herbs or powdered sugar will not only garnish the roll but also camouflage any imperfections.

ROULADE FLAVORINGS AND FILLINGS

Many flavorings can be added to the flat soufflé. Add 1½ to 2 cups grated cheese, or finely chopped and cooked spinach, or onions to the base before adding the egg whites.

Served hot, the flavored roulade then wraps deliciously around such fillings as curried shrimp, lobster Newburg, mussels in a cream sauce, sweetbreads in a velouté, or beef tips or mushrooms in sauce Robert.

A roulade is fine served cold with fillings of crabmeat, cold spinach mousse or creamed cheese, capers and salmon. Your options are limited only by your imagination and what is in your larder.

Remember, the filling should be thick since you will *roll* the roulade. Make more sauce than is needed for the filling and serve the extra sauce as a topping for the roulade, or make another sauce that complements the filling.

The Savory Roulade

Serves 6 as a main course Serves 8 to 10 as an hors d'oeuvre

6 tablespoons butter
½ cup flour
2 cups milk
6 egg yolks
½ teaspoon salt
6 egg whites
⅛ teaspoon salt
¼ teaspoon cream of tartar (if not using a copper bowl)

Preheat oven to 325 degrees and place oven rack in the upper third of the oven.

Prepare a 10-by-17-inch jelly-roll pan (see page 73).

Melt the butter over medium heat in a saucepan. Do not allow to brown. Remove the pan from the burner, add the flour to make a roux and whisk to incorporate thoroughly. Return to the burner and cook at medium temperature for about 1 minute. Do not brown the roux.

Remove from the heat, gradually add the milk and blend with a whisk. Return to medium-high heat and bring to a boil, whisking constantly. Boil for 1 minute, whisking to make a thick sauce.

Remove from heat and whisk to cool mixture for about a minute. Add the egg yolks, whisking them in one at a time. Add the ½ teaspoon salt.

Beat the egg whites in a clean, dry bowl with ⅛ teaspoon salt and ¼ teaspoon optional cream of tartar. When the whites stand in stiff, moist peaks, fold about a cup of the whites into the warm base to lighten it. Then fold the base into the egg whites. Fold together lightly to incorporate.

Pour the roulade mixture into the prepared jelly-roll pan and smooth to distribute it evenly. Bake in the upper third of the oven for about 30 minutes or until the roulade has puffed and feels springy in the middle.

Remove from the oven and place the pan on a cake rack to cool for 5 minutes. Turn the roulade out onto wax paper (see page 73). Then peel off the baked wax paper on top.

When the roulade has cooled, spread it with the filling and roll it onto a serving platter. Serve immediately.

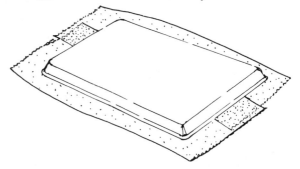

Chicken Liver Filling with Madeira Sauce

A splendid sample filling for the plain savory roulade.

4 tablespoons butter
2 pounds uncooked chicken livers,
quartered
4 scallions, whites and tops,
chopped
1½ cups fresh chopped mushrooms
½ teaspoon salt
¼ teaspoon pepper
½ cup brandy
2 cups Madeira sauce (see following
recipe)

Heat the butter in a saucepan. When bubbling hot, add the chicken livers and cook until they are lightly browned and pink in the center. Add the scallions, mushrooms and seasonings. Cook for 1 more minute. Flame with brandy.

When the flames have subsided, remove the liver mixture from the heat. Add enough Madeira sauce to completely coat the liver mixture—about ½ cup. Reserve the remainder of the sauce for a topping.

NOTE: To flame the chicken livers, warm the brandy in a small pan (do not boil) and touch it with a lighted match. Pour the flames over the chicken livers.

SIMPLE MADEIRA SAUCE

2 tablespoons butter
3 tablespoons flour
2 cups beef broth
1 cup Madeira
2 tablespoons chopped fresh parsley,
   or 2 teaspoons dried
1 bay leaf
2 tablespoons chopped fresh thyme,
   or 2 teaspoons dried

Melt the butter in a small saucepan. Remove from burner. Add flour, and whisk to incorporate thoroughly. Return to burner and cook at medium-high temperature, whisking occasionally until the mixture browns. Whisk in the stock, Madeira, herbs and seasonings, and bring to a boil, whisking frequently. Simmer, uncovered, for 30 minutes. The sauce should reduce to 2 cups. Taste the sauce and add salt if necessary.

Cheese and Herb Roulade with Creamed Mushroom Filling

Made in exactly the same way as the basic recipe, this roulade is flavored with the cheese and herbs of your choice and can incorporate a variety of savory fillings. The cheese and herbs are added at the point when you add the egg whites to the base.

This creamy mushroom filling is tasty in either the plain or the cheese roulade.

SAVORY ROULADE WITH CHEESE AND HERBS

1 cup grated cheese (Gruyère,
   Parmesan, or cheddar for an
   American flavor)
2 tablespoons chopped fresh chives,
   tarragon, or dill weed

CREAMED MUSHROOM FILLING

8 tablespoons butter
½ cup scallions, whites and tops, cut
   in julienne strips
2 cups sliced fresh mushrooms
½ cup flour
2 cups chicken stock
2 tablespoons vermouth
½ teaspoon salt
1 tablespoon fresh chopped chives or
   frozen chives, thawed
¼ cup grated Gruyère cheese

Melt the butter in a saucepan over medium heat. Do not allow to brown. Cook the scallions for 2 minutes. Add the mushrooms and cook for 1 minute.

Remove from the burner. Add flour to make a roux and whisk to incorporate thoroughly.

Return to the burner and cook over medium heat for about 1 minute. Do not brown the roux.

Remove from heat, gradually add the chicken stock and vermouth, and blend with a whisk. Return to medium-high heat and bring to a boil, whisking constantly. Boil for 1 minute, whisking to make a thick sauce. Remove from heat and whisk in the salt, chives and Gruyère cheese. Combine and correct seasoning if necessary.

NOTE: This filling is good in an omelette, too.

The Sweet Roulade

Most sweet roulades are made in exactly the same way as savory roulades, save that the salt is omitted. You may fill these sweet roulades with any sweet fillings such as crème pâtissière (page 26), fresh fruit, or crème chantilly (page 79) and fruit. Then top with a fruit sauce (page 67), if you wish.

Chocolate Roulade with Crème Chantilly   *Serves 8 to 10*

Through much experimentation with chocolate roulades, I have concluded that, like chocolate soufflés, roulades are too thick and moist when made with a cream sauce base. I have also worked with chocolate recipes that used no flour at all. These recipes tend to be too soggy as well. Instead of either of these alternatives, use the following bouillie base to make a lighter chocolate roulade.

½ cup cornstarch
2 cups milk
6 egg yolks
1 cup sugar
½ teaspoon salt
6 ounces semi-sweet chocolate bits
1 teaspoon vanilla
6 egg whites
⅛ teaspoon salt
¼ teaspoon cream of tartar (if not using a copper bowl)
1 tablespoon unsweetened powdered cocoa
1 tablespoon powdered sugar
2 cups or more Crème Chantilly

Preheat oven to 325 degrees. Place rack in the upper third of the oven.

Prepare a 10-by-17-inch jelly-roll pan (see page 73).

Put ½ cup of cornstarch in a medium-sized saucepan. Add ½ cup of milk; whisk until smooth. Then add the remaining milk. Cook over medium-high heat, whisking rapidly until the mixture is smooth and very thick.

Remove from heat and cool for a minute so that the yolks do not poach when they are added. Add the egg yolks one at a time and stir until well blended. Add sugar and ½ teaspoon salt, and stir until well blended. Add chocolate bits and stir until chocolate melts. Add 1 teaspoon of vanilla and mix well.

Beat the egg whites with ⅛ teaspoon salt and ¼ teaspoon optional cream of tartar until soft peaks form. Sprinkle with 1 tablespoon of sugar and beat until stiff, moist peaks form. Fold 1 cup whites into the warm base to lighten it. Then pour the sauce into the whites, folding lightly with a large whisk, and be careful not to deflate the whites.

Pour the mixture into a prepared jelly-roll pan and spread evenly with a rubber spatula to distribute the mixture.

Bake in the upper third of the oven about 40 minutes or until the roulade has puffed and springs back when lightly touched.

Remove from oven and cool the pan on a rack for 5 minutes. Turn the roulade out onto wax paper. Then peel the baked wax paper from the top.

When the roulade has cooled, spread it with Crème Chantilly and roll it onto a serving platter. Combine 1 tablespoon unsweetened cocoa and 1 tablespoon powdered sugar. Place in a sieve and dust the top of the roll. Refrigerate the roulade if you are not serving it immediately.

CRÈME CHANTILLY

Makes at least 4 cups

2 cups whipping cream, cold
2 tablespoons sugar
2 teaspoons vanilla extract or
 2 tablespoons brandy, rum or
 sweet liqueur

Pour the cream into a chilled bowl and whip it briefly before adding the sugar. Then whip it until it is thick and fluffy. The whisk or beater will leave light traces on the surface of the cream and the cream will retain its shape lightly. Fold in the flavoring. If the cream is to be piped into rosettes, whip it until just stiff.

Pseudo-Soufflés

A cold soufflé is an impostor, not a true soufflé. It certainly looks like one, standing high above the rim of its dish. But the cold soufflé is playing dress-up. Its proud posture results from the fact that it is too big for its bowl, not from the expansion of cooked, beaten egg whites. A collar around the soufflé dish of a cold soufflé creates a supporting mold for the excess mixture. So when the soufflé has set and the collar is removed, the soufflé appears to have risen.

A cold soufflé is basically a mousse into which beaten egg whites have been folded. These egg whites lighten the mousse and make it less rich. Sometimes extra whites are added.

To make a cold soufflé, make a base of egg yolks. Add sugar and other flavorings. Then add beaten egg whites for lightness and whipped cream for richness. Hold it all together with gelatin.

Cold soufflés are easy to make and they always receive rave reviews. Their light, creamy texture and their spectacular appearance make them seem quite evanescent, when actually they could have been waiting patiently in your freezer for weeks. Stash several away for a busy day. You will sleep better for it.

Cold Raspberry Soufflé

Serves 6 to 8

This recipe is basic to all the cold soufflés in this book. Only the flavoring changes. Be sure to see the section on whisking egg whites and folding whites and yolks together (pages 38-40).

LIQUID AND YOLKS:
1 package gelatin
¼ cup liquid: juice from the raspberries, orange juice or water
5 egg yolks

FLAVORINGS:
½ cup sugar
1 cup pureed or chopped raspberries, or 2 10-ounce packages frozen berries, drained
2 tablespoons framboise or Grand Marnier

CREAM AND WHITES:
2 cups whipping cream
5 egg whites
1 tablespoon sugar
¼ teaspoon cream of tartar (if not using a copper bowl)
⅛ teaspoon salt

Prepare a 1-quart soufflé dish by putting a collar around it and wiping it with an oiled paper towel.

Sprinkle the gelatin on the ¼ cup of liquid in a small saucepan.

Beat the egg yolks until frothy. Gradually add the ½ cup of sugar. Continue beating until the mixture is thick and mousse-like (see page 40). Fold in the remaining flavorings.

Whip the cream until it is the same consistency as the egg yolks and sugar. Beating until the cream is stiff will make it hard to incorporate.

Check the gelatin. It should look like grainy jello. Place the gelatin over extremely low heat to melt.

Meanwhile, whisk the whites, salt and optional cream of tartar to the soft peak stage (see page 39). Add the 1 tablespoon sugar and whisk to moist, stiff peaks.

Pour the melted gelatin into the yolk mixture. Fold in the egg whites. Finally, fold in the whipped cream.

Pour the mixture into a prepared soufflé dish. Refrigerate for at least 3 hours to set. If freezing, refrigerate for 1 hour. Then wrap and freeze.

NOTE: If the gelatin gets too hot, it may fail to gel or will become stringy and clump together. It must be melted over extremely low heat, so try a simple test to be sure that the gelatin is not too hot. Periodically, remove the pan from the heat and place it on your hand. If the pan is too hot for your hand, it is too hot for the gelatin. If your gelatin is too hot you will not forget it!

Variations on the Cold Raspberry Soufflé

Substitute the following flavorings and liquids for the flavoring and liquid in the Cold Raspberry Soufflé.

COLD CITRUS SOUFFLÉ

LIQUID:
¼ cup rum

FLAVORING:
1½ cups sugar
¼ cup lemon juice
¼ cup lime juice
Zest of 1 lemon
Zest of 2 limes

DECORATION: Lemon twists

COLD COFFEE SOUFFLÉ

LIQUID:
¼ cup coffee

FLAVORINGS:
½ cup sugar
½ cup double-strength coffee
2 tablespoons Kahlua
1 teaspoon vanilla

DECORATION: Whipped cream rosettes

COLD PINEAPPLE SOUFFLÉ

LIQUID:
¼ cup water

FLAVORING:
¾ cup sugar
2 cups drained, crushed pineapple
¼ cup kirsch
2 tablespoons lemon juice

DECORATION: Fresh mint leaves